BRIDGES TO THE WORLD

BRIDGES TO THE WORLD

Edited by

Harold K. Bales

tidings

1908 Grand Avenue
Nashville, Tennessee 37203

Library of Congress Catalog Card Number: 75-171884
© 1971 by TIDINGS, 1908 Grand Avenue
Nashville, Tennessee 37203
EV002B

CONTENTS

PREFACE

On January 4, 1971, the United Methodist Congress on Evangelism convened in New Orleans, Louisiana. In a five-day collage of addresses, workshops, worship experiences, and experimental events hundreds of United Methodist clergy and laymen sought new directions for a bold, contemporary evangelism ministry. An important part of the Congress on Evangelism was the National Conference on New Styles in Cooperative Evangelism under the leadership of the Reverend Joe Hale. The primary focus of this conference was Key 73, an exciting strategy for cooperative evangelism just then in the developmental stage. Here was a significant event with broad implications not only for United Methodists but for all Christians. The aim: to communicate Christ to America through a major, pan-denominational, evangelical thrust in 1973. It is out of this conference and in support of this venture in faith that this book is offered.

The chapters in this volume are portions of addresses by the very able resource persons to the conference. They are offered in the hope that they may provide insight and inspiration for those who seek an expanded evangelism ministry. Local churches may find clues to greater corporate commitment here. Individual Christians may be prompted to new pathways on their personal pilgrimage. Questions are added to each chapter for those persons and small groups who will risk further reflection and involvement. This is a resource for reconciliation. May it help you in your ministry of reconciliation.

A special note of appreciation is due Joe Hale for his leadership in the Conference on New Styles in Cooperative Evangelism. His further contributions to the making of this book were invaluable. The patient help of Misses Hilda Young, Ada McKinley, Floibelle Wise and Mrs. Edward Pugh with this manuscript is acknowledged with gratitude.

7

I am most grateful to the contributors to this volume and to the conference out of which it comes. May their insight and commitment to a ministry of evangelism be multiplied in all who read their words.

H. B.
May 15, 1971
Nashville, Tennessee

INTRODUCTION

The New Testament speaks of two kinds of time: *chronos* and *kairos*. Chronos refers to time which flows on second after second, building to minutes, hours, days, weeks, months, years. It has no particular qualities about it, except that it continues, season following season.

Kairos is a qualitative term. In its simplest form it means the fullness of time. A particular moment in history when many factors or events coincide to make it a pivotal point in history. This is the term used by the New Testament writers to describe the birth of Christ—not simply a date, but the fullness of time.

Kairos is not limited to a single event, but is responsibly used to describe many times in history when time was in *fullness*. Historians are quick to look back and identify for us the times as well as the causes and effects of such kairos moments.

I believe that we are living in a kairos time. It is a special challenge, and shifts of accent and emphasis. And the way in which we live in and through it, as well as the decisions we make in terms of our real priorities will be of extreme importance for all future generations.

The greatest issue before us is the world's challenge to what we have proclaimed for centuries: "Jesus Christ is Lord."

To confess him as Savior is indeed personally comforting, but to claim him as Lord in the midst of a cultural pluralism is more easily spoken than practiced. Yet at the same time numerous laymen and pastors today are attempting to move out of the life of the (institutional) church as a sign of their need to more dynamically witness to their faith in Christ. How shall we celebrate his Lordship and our salvation?

Just prior to World War II, there was considerable concern in the United States about a possible invasion on the Atlantic coast. In defense, a series of coastal gun emplacements were built. The uniqueness of these guns was their retractability.

9

Hidden behind large bunkers, they would lift into place, discharge their shells, and retract into a hidden position till the time for the next shot. The times will not allow for this style of Christianity, firing only when convenient and retracting to safe havens while the battle rages.

Celebration of salvation is not limited to worship, prayer, and the sacraments; rather it must include our whole lives. We must learn to really live in the freedom that Christ offers to us.

The New Testament is filled with accounts of persons who were set free and so celebrated. Peter, James, John, and other of the disciples, Paul, Silas, Timothy, Barnabas, and the list could go on. The life and history of the church would fill many pages with the names of others.

And today is not without its witnesses.

Some time ago I was on the west coast sharing in a conference program. I met a young woman, the mother of four children. She told me how she graduated from high school and immediately married. Then came the children in rapid succession providing her with a busy and hectic life. Taking stock of her life, she said, "I never really pursued a formal education. In fact, when I take inventory of my life, about all I know how to do is change diapers and wipe runny noses. But the miracle of it is that I survived those years and it seemed like all of a sudden the kids were in school and for the first time in my life I had some discretionary time."

With the children in school from 9 A.M. to 3:30 P.M. she was free to make some decisions about how she might use this time. Because of her Christian commitment, she felt a responsibility to be a good steward of this new freedom. "I began to look around because I believe that in my relationship to Jesus Christ I, too, have a ministry. But what was I equipped to do? How could I serve?"

Her search for ministry brought her in contact with an institution for the care of children who were essentially little more than human vegetables—"whose physical needs were such that . . . well, they really needed someone to change diapers and wipe runny noses." Then she said, "I have been going to the hospital while school is in session . . . but that is

not really what I want to tell you. The interesting thing is that
when I go to church, because some people have learned what
I am doing, they say, 'You'll get a star in your crown for
that!' and the hardest thing I have to explain is that I'm really
not trying to earn brownie points: what I am really doing is
celebrating my salvation."

If the mandate of our Lord is to go and make disciples,
then the time is upon us when we will either respond with
obedience or deny him by default. If we choose to build *bridges
to the world* we will meet both a challenge and a risk. The
challenge is to lay aside some of the old formulas that are no
longer adequate for our day and risk beginning a pilgrimage
into an unknown future. If I choose, for instance, to get to
know, share, and work together with some other Christians
who operate under a different denominational label or theological perspective there is always the risk that my personal position may be altered. I may be challenged more than I am able
to challenge. Yet, it seems to me, we must not simply choose
to do those things that are comfortable for us. To take that
route means we have decided to cease growing and have
started to feed primarily upon our past experiences, a practice
that is contradictory to the action of God in history who is
constantly moving toward the future.

We need bridges to the world! As the man Jesus Christ
was God's bridge of redemption and new birth, we, too, have
a ministry of reconciling love.

To this end Christ calls us. Let us celebrate our salvation
with him in this kairos time.

That's when the action really is—celebrating our salvation.
In the fullness of these times, we celebrate our salvation. If
there are to be *bridges to the world* we must respond to Christ
with our whole lives.

As individuals and congregations we must bridge ways to
the person who is outside the Christian community, to the
lonely, forgotten persons who may live close by our door with
whom the good news of Christ has never been shared and
appropriated.

We must find a way to celebrate our faith and declare salvation through the media, with literally thousands of radio and

television stations, and local, suburban, and regional newspapers employed from the local church base. And at the same time in our day-to-day living, we can deliberately place our lives in those places where a word and witness can be so shared that individuals are open to change and new depths of commitment and service.

Thus, in our time, we may for God's sake become *bridges to the world.*

JOSEPH H. YEAKEL

1

Communicating Christ As a Changing Church in a Changing World

By Bruce Larson

The world is changing. The church is changing. Communication is changing.

These facts are obvious. But we must face them honestly, without illusion, and see how they interrelate if we are to be effective in communicating Christ and life.

There is nothing unusual about change. What's more, change is inevitable. Yet we in the church often find ourselves resisting change as if all the greatest and best things happened long ago and it is our duty to preserve or recapture them.

In earlier, simpler times, it was perhaps possible to live with a sense of stability and order. In a lifetime you might not see tremendous differences, if you lived with a certain level of experience and continuity in society, community, worship, liturgy.

Now that is no longer possible. Every few years we see amazing things taking place: scientific advances, shifts in the power structure, social and economic upheavals, a profound shaking of the whole order of things. The rate of change is fantastic. One of today's best-sellers, *Future Shock,* is devoted to the difficulties human beings have in assimilating cataclysmic changes.

As the father of three teen-agers, I find it hard to grasp

13

the cultural revolution that is their normal way of life. But even if I were only twenty-five, I suspect I would be "out of it." Someone has said that young people today live as though the bomb had already dropped. The Now Generation is in profound ways different from all preceding generations.

Their vocabulary is different. Their education is different: electronic rather than linear. Their music is different. They are oriented to films, not books. They are seeking a life-style that rejects gender stereotypes. They want no part of traditional prejudices—though some of their own prejudices are equally irrational. They want the simple life: organic foods, and clothes that look as if they had not been made by machines.

Perhaps most profoundly, they are not impressed by words. This puts a heavy burden on my generation. For us, talk has been everything—in the church, in the universities, in politics. Someone has guessed that if Michelangelo were alive today he couldn't get a degree in art because he could not verbalize his art. He could paint, but that would not be enough for us: he would have to define, analyze, and perhaps teach what he did. Our whole approach to life has been semantic—in the church, in education, in therapy.

This won't do for tomorrow's adults. They have a "show-me" attitude. We are moving into an incarnational era where *demonstrations* of love, involvement, and caring are essential.

Look at youth's banners; listen to their slogans. What do you find? Love, peace, joy. Interesting. Those are the first three "fruits of the Spirit." Young people have picked them up—perhaps unconsciously—as the hallmarks of what they want to be and do.

In other words, we find ourselves in a new cultural climate which is profoundly spiritual. We who are older have talked a lot about the fruits of the Spirit, but we have not invested our lives in love, peace, and joy. Rather, we have sought things, place, privilege, status, early retirement.

The world is outdoing the church in some of its desired or realized goals.

In my youth, it was considered very square to talk about Jesus Christ. You could say, "Come to church with me." That was all right, for everybody went to some church. Just as long as you didn't take Jesus Christ too seriously.

Today, any talk about church with kids is "out." But talk about Jesus and you are "in." The sound of "Jesus Christ, Superstar" blares from every transistor radio, and on the West Coast thousands of youngsters are "turning on" Jesus in a revival that may well sweep the nation.

There are two ways you can look at what is happening. You can see a tremendous change taking place in the church and say that we are in a "post-Christian" era: that Christendom is on the way out. Or you can say that we are really in a "pre-Christian" era. I believe the latter to be the case, though I can't defend my opinion except intuitively.

It seems to me that God has allowed a great deal of experimentation to take place in the last two thousand years—a very short space of time in the history of the world. That is, I look at what happened to and through the patristic fathers, the early councils, St. Francis of Assisi, the Augustinians, Martin Luther, the Wesleys, and many others, and I see their achievements as attempts to create working models—creaking along and doing some fantastic things. But I don't believe that the thing we read about in Revelation—a new heaven and a new earth and God in tune with his people—has really happened yet.

True, there have been some great individuals and experimental communities along the line, but I believe that what God had in mind in sending Jesus Christ is still to happen, and that we are a part of something bigger than a new reformation. It may be the real beginning of the Christian church.

We are witnessing the death of ecclesiasticism, the death of Christendom. But perhaps "Christendom" is not what God had in mind in the first place.

If we can be free of having to defend Christendom, and can go out to the world and talk about Jesus and not about Christianity, we have a whole new stance. We can talk about Jesus Christ and man and need and grace and hope. But if we think we must defend the past two thousand years, even though there are good "kernels" and great achievements, we must apologize for an awful lot of junk: crusades, inquisi-

tions, witch-burnings, bigotry, injustice, not to mention reaction, defense of the status quo, anti-intellectualism, interference with progress, and a host of other evils.

I hear a man say, "Of course I'm a Christian, but as for
the church. . . ." And I'm with him. Most of us are. We are
glad to see the church changing in hopeful ways.

New forms are coming. A long time ago, Seneca said, "If
a man doesn't know to which harbor he is sailing, every wind
that blows is the wrong wind." Conversely, when you have
an idea where you are going, any wind that blows can somehow move the craft along. You can tack, breach, adjust your
sails, and take advantage of whatever comes along. I doubt
that God will adjust the "cultural winds," but this need not
dismay his people. Not if we have a sense of where we are
going, an eye on the goal.

New moralities? Why should we fear them? We can analyze
them, adjust, take stock of what is happening, and sail right
on. New forms scare a lot of people, perhaps because the forms
themselves have become the end product. That's pretty sick.

The winds of change are blowing across the land, and a lot
of things are being shaken up. But most of them are not biblical concepts at all. Most of them are cultural patterns that
have been picked up along the way and can well be discarded.

One Sunday morning in an old church out in Nebraska, a
kind of "nameless Gothic" structure where a congregation of
Presbyterians gathers for worship, a most unusual thing occurred.

Someone had come up with the idea of using balloons—
helium-filled balloons—to represent praise and thanksgiving
to God. Everyone entering the church that morning was given
a balloon. The congregation was told, "Any time you feel like
it, let your balloon go, and that will represent your saying
silently, but visibly, 'Praise God,' or 'Thank you, God,' or
'Here's my prayer going up.' "

All through the service balloons kept floating up, and each
time it happened it seemed as if someone was saying, "Hey,
that's great, Lord. Thank you." Of course, they were Presbyterians, and at the end of the service about one-third of the

people were still clutching their balloons. But that was all right. Freedom!

And think about the music we are starting to sing now in church. We are not discarding the great biblical Psalms, but the hymns of the seventeenth, eighteenth, and nineteenth centuries. And we are writing songs about what God is doing right now. At least this is happening in some places, and I'm delighted.

One of the features of the Wesleyan revolution was that they dared to believe that you could sing about the mighty acts of God among his people in the here and now. I think that if the Wesleys came back physically today they would be appalled to discover that we are still singing the hymns they wrote. It was not their intention to set a pattern for all time. The idea was that hymn-writers in a continually changing church, experiencing grace in new ways through Christ, could say, "This is happening, and this." Somehow we have taken their revolutionary breakthrough and bound it within the pages of a standard hymnbook.

What's wrong with composing new choruses of prayer and praise? People object that the new might not be "theologically sound." Well, so what? The church has survived two thousand years of theological un-soundness. The more important question is, does the hymn express what God is doing now through his people?

I have visited churches where mimeographed sheets of music were passed out—popular tunes with new words that someone in the church had composed that very week. A healing had taken place, or a reconciliation, or the city council had written a hymn about it. Imagine that you are a visitor in that church under those circumstances: wouldn't it say something powerful to you about the love of God? Wouldn't it be more thrilling than singing a hymn by Charles Wesley—great as his hymns are?

Let's talk about pews. On Youth Sunday, one church in our town asked its Junior High group to conduct the morning worship service. It happened that a new sanctuary was being built and the pews had not yet been screwed into place. The kids planning the service asked themselves if there was anything sacred about staring at the backs of people's necks during the worship service. They could think of no good reason, scriptural, or otherwise, to preserve this pattern.

They rearranged all the pews so that no two of them were in a straight line, and so that people could face each other while they worshipped. Revolutionary idea!

I'm glad to report that the elders in that church were free enough to say, "Before we screw these pews down, let's leave them like this for a few months and see how it feels to look at faces and not the backs of necks while we worship Jesus Christ."

I am suggesting that such innovations need not be feared. They represent people struggling with the whole biblical heritage in twentieth century forms. Why candles and incense and not balloons? Why pews in a row? Why pews at all? Can you defend them?

Where else in our world do you find rows of pews? Theatres don't have them. Auditoriums don't have them. Schools don't have them. Even funeral homes don't have them.

What I am saying is that the emerging church is throwing out a lot of things in its worship, but it is not throwing out what is biblical. It is throwing out cultural "branches."

What is left is the Lord Jesus Christ and some needy people reminding themselves that he is present with grace and that they can affirm what he is doing.

We see new goals for the church. We are not talking about "religion" any more, or "churchmanship," or even "goodness."

Jesus Christ talked about *life*. He came that we might have life, and that he might make us free, that his joy might be in us.

We are coming to see that perhaps the most important ministry we have as a church is to one another. I hear Jesus saying to Peter, "You've followed me; committed your life to me. You've left home and family and business. You have been out preaching the gospel, raising the dead, healing the sick, doing all the fantastic things. But the harder thing is yet to come. When you have been converted, strengthen the brethren."

You and I know that the hardest thing, the most relevant thing the church can do is to be a healing force for one another. To be channels of life, wholeness, freedom, healing, joy, fulfillment. .

Judgment has come on the church because we have not been concerned about people becoming fulfilled as people, able to communicate, and love, and become involved, and risk, and discover potentialities. We have focused on negatives: getting over a drinking problem, dealing with your inferiority complex. When you focus on the negatives, you end up with religion, not life.

In this changing church, we are discovering a new center which many of us clergy over thirty-five are not equipped to handle because of our training. The new center of the church's ministry is the laity. Not just the laity who pay the bills and offer an occasional prayer for the "professionals" whose task it is to do the job. No: this new laity is a royal priesthood called forth by God.

The reason for this development is quite obvious. If you believe that God cares about the world and wants to provide healing for people, mentally, physically, emotionally, and socially, and if you begin to sense the deep needs all around, you will realize that there aren't enough clergy, psychiatrists, medical doctors, therapists, counselors—even if all of them were doing a maximum job—to begin to touch the world's needs. The royal priesthood of the church, wherein everyone is a minister, is essential.

Part of our problem in the past has been that those who were truly concerned tended to become polarized into two groups. There were the scalp hunters: evangelists who went around buttonholing people with the "Brother, are you saved?" approach. And there were those who were concerned about the cup of cold water: the jails and prisons, the dispossessed, those who were exploited economically and socially. In other words, the social action crowd.

Whenever you begin to have polarized ministries, I believe you have a very sick church and a very sick people.

The layman, I think, is meant to be an evangelist in some situations, where he can simply build relationships with people over a period of weeks, months, or years. Then when someone says, "What can I do?" the evangelist has earned the right to say, "Well, when I was in that spot I turned my life over to Somebody else and asked for help."

At this point he can help the other person accept Christ and begin the great adventure.

The same layman, in a different situation, can be a reconciler or healer between two fellow Christians. Suppose a husband and wife are not making it in their marriage; their brother can step in and become a priest—a "little Christ"— to them. Everywhere there are rifts: between parent and child, between co-workers, between friends, between factions in a church council or community. Laymen can learn to be not only evangelists but also reconcilers: those through whom others can listen and begin to hear each other.

Further: those laymen who are adept at evangelism and reconciliation can also become involved in prophetic action. And by that I mean social action.

What is social action, after all? It is simply discerning— as did the prophets of old—where some structure in business or society or government is hurting people and stepping in to initiate some corrective action. When the government first began to move against segregation there was resistance.

But in one southern town four churchmen, without any fanfare, began to talk to their clergy and local businessmen about reasonable compliance with the law. Within months, this town of thirty or thirty-five thousand people had abandoned institutionalized segregation and was at least nominally integrated.

Because of four men—a Roman Catholic, a Southern Presbyterian, a Methodist, and a Southern Baptist—who ate lunch together, played golf together, and prayed together, the climate of an entire community was peacefully changed.

I should add that of these four men, one was the owner of a big mill, one was the president of the biggest local bank, one headed a small but influential prep school, and one was the commander of a naval base with a big payroll in the town. They had power. They had influence. They were not afraid to use it prophetically as Christians, and as four citizens they accomplished what the corporate church could never have accomplished by passing resolutions and issuing decrees.

Every Christian has his own place of power and prestige, whether in education, politics, business, law, neighborhood associations, or what have you. The thing is, we don't wait for God to give us some new kind of power. If we are God's people, we take the secular power we already have, get a coalition together, and begin to move. This is biblical; this is prophetic. Perhaps if we stop calling it "social action" and start to call it "prophetic action," we will turn off fewer people and get more done.

To see a church where the laity, conscious of their power, charisma, and calling, become evangelists, healers, and prophetic activists, is to see changes in the shape of a town, a state, or a nation.

This laity is the new center of the church's ministry. You who are laymen will have to be patient with us who are the clergy. We are not well equipped to help you do this. We may believe you ought to do this, but we must work together to find out how.

The new message of the church is a combination of two things that have been separated far too long. We have to say to the world that Jesus Christ is alive; that he is Lord and has healing in his hands; that he can transform life. But we must be able to tell the world that Jesus Christ has come to live in some very strange people who are just like them. This means we have to talk about our own humanity. "We have this treasure in earthen vessels." We inside the church are just like those on the outside.

In the past, the church has either identified too strongly with the world and tended to forget the Divinity, or it has talked too much about Jesus with the implication that "we are just like him." And that's not true. The biblical message is that we are free to be ourselves, unashamed to be strange and peculiar—"earthen vessels."

As church people we are *not* called to be "like Jesus." This is a misconception we have labored under which has made evangelism terribly difficult. We are not to copy Jesus.

You only copy someone when he is not present. If you have a friend with a marvelous sense of humor who tells great stories, you may try to repeat his stories and be like him when you move into a setting where he is not known. But if you try to do it when he is present, you only make a fool of yourself.

The church is not to copy Jesus because *he is here.* Every time we try to pretend we are like him we say, in effect, "He used to be here and if you look at us you will see what he was like." Nonsense.

Another variation on this theme is this stance: "We used to be terrible people; then we accepted Christ and now we sing hymns, pray, do visitation work," and so on.

This leaves out the fact that we still fight with our kids, have the sulks, get touchy at the office, neglect our wives, get depressed and lonely.

Christians get lonely just like everyone else. The difference is that we know what to do with our loneliness. We can share it. The church then becomes a fellowship of people who are unashamed of failure, unafraid to be alone, willing to be human. We talk about Jesus Christ being gracious enough to come and live in us.

Some time ago I took part in a seminar with Paul Tournier, the psychiatrist, medical doctor, and author of many great books. During one of the sessions, someone asked Dr. Tournier, "Is it possible to be a phony Christian?" When this question was translated by our interpreter from English into French, Paul Tournier smiled and said, "Mais oui. C'est moi." ("Of course. It's me.")

He went on to admit that sometimes he tries to be the person people think he is after reading his books. Seeing this, his wife says, "Paul, you've done it again. I can see it. You're trying to play God in people's lives."

"She's right, you know," Tournier acknowledged. Then he opened up and told us about himself, from his feet of clay right up to his Adam's apple.

The most marvelous thing happened as he spoke. Christ in him reached out and lifted our spirits. For if Paul Tournier can be like this—human, fallible—there is hope for all of us.

This is the kind of ministry we must find in the emerging church: Christ using us even in our weakness. More: using our weakness.

How do we communicate this?

If we take the Bible seriously, we find that man's basic problem is not his sin, rebelliousness, deviousness. God has already dealt with our rebellious acts.

The issue—from Genesis 3 right up to the present—is a breakdown in communication. People have always found ways of covering themselves with fig leaves and getting behind the bushes. Today we call these "defense mechanisms." And the best place to make use of them is in the church. If you get busy enough in church work—humanitarian work, "doing good," running for office—God will never find you. And if he did, you'd have excuses, evasions, and comfortable lies to gloss over the confrontation.

"Where is your brother?" God asked Cain.

"How do I know? Am I my brother's keeper?" Up goes the barrier.

I wonder what would have happened if Cain had been honest enough to say, "I killed him. I couldn't stand him. You always liked him better than me, God."

Throughout the biblical record and throughout history the story does not change. God did have a plan, and in time Jesus came; our sin was dealt with. But the lingering problem is the problem of communication. We just can't seem to tell it like it is."

Moses leads his people out of Egypt. But after wandering in the wilderness they begin to think they might have been better off as slaves of the Pharaoh. Moses goes up to the mountaintop and God speaks. "Go tell my people to climb the mountain," God says to Moses, "and I will explain the purpose of all this."

"Follow me up the mountain," Moses urges the Israelites.

What is their reaction? "Oh, no, preacher, we're not good enough to go up there. We're just ordinary, humble folk. You go back and listen to God, and then on Sunday morning you can get up in the pulpit and tell us what he said."

This has been the church game ever since. If we dared to go up the mountain, meet God face to face, and hear him say, "This is my plan for you," we would have no hiding place.

But if we get the message secondhand, we can always argue with the preacher.

I'm suggesting that the new church is going to be people who are free to face the facts and say, "This is the game. This is the hiding place. This is the cop-out."

To reach this point may involve a painful process. We can start by facing honestly our own attitudes to life, God, and ourselves.

First, let us acknowledge that most of us basically are either talkers or doers. Either we act things out without talking much about them, or we verbalize without following through with action. Remember the parable about the man with two sons? One of them said Yes, but didn't do the job; the other said No, but later changed his mind and obeyed his father.

The musical play "Fiddler on the Roof" has a marvelous scene that illustrates these two attitudes perfectly. Tevye, a fat, middle-aged, faithful, harassed Jewish peasant living in Russia toward the end of the nineteenth century, turns to Golde, his wife of many years and asks, "Do you love me?"

"Do I love you? What a question!" Who, Golde asks, has been keeping his house, caring for his children, feeding his chickens, and sharing his bed all this time?

"But do you love me?" Tevye persists.

Back and forth goes the conversation, without any resolution. Tevye must have Golde's love articulated; she can't articulate it. He is a talker—she is a doer.

Christ says to each of us: "Listen. If you are going to be able to relate to your husband or wife or children or co-workers or neighbors or the people half-way round the world, you've got to get out of your bag of being a doer or a talker. I want to make you a whole person—to fulfill the dimension that is strange for you." And if we are willing, he does precisely this, making communication possible where before it was impossible.

Second, let's admit that we are usually either givers or receivers. Max Beerbohm said that the world is divided into two classes of people: the hosts and the guests. The guest is one who sits down and says, "Well, when do we eat? What's next? What's for entertainment?"

Some of us, it seems, always expect to be taken care of, entertained, and amused. "How was church this week?" "Well, the sermon wasn't so good. The choir sang off-key. Too many candles."

But a "giver" may be just as sick as a chronic "receiver." If you can't receive from people, it's unlikely that you can receive from God—and God has something to give you.

Both givers and receivers have their problems. God wants to set us free to be both.

Third, and most painful, we must accept the fact that the world is made up of the blessed and the unblessed.

I heard Karl Olsson give a series of lectures on this point, and suddenly I realized that the Bible takes it very seriously indeed. Every family has its "Joseph," and the other brothers grind their teeth because just one has the blessing of the parents. All the children may be loved equally, yet one has a place of special favor. Who can tell why?

And sometimes we parents, realizing that we have "blessed" one child, feel guilty and show more love to the others. It is as if we had no control over the situation.

Remember Esau and Jacob. Esau was the blessed: the father's boy, the hunter, the hairy one. Jacob was unblessed, but he and his mother tricked the father into reversing the sons' roles. It was not to gain the inheritance; it was something more intangible.

This is all part of being human; it's the name of the game.

The prodigal son knows he is blessed; he is free to take off and run away from his responsibilities. The blessed tend to be irresponsible. The unblessed are those who stay home, work hard, care for their parents, go to seminary, support the establishment. Life for them is grim. The unblessed ones who become preachers spend a lot of time sermonizing on the Cross, but it may be thinly-veiled preaching about their own unblessedness.

Humanly, there is little to be done about this phenomenon, but with God it is possible. When Jesus Christ says to us, "Look, there are those who are near and those who are far, but all are brought close together in my blood," that is the remedy. In Jesus Christ we find release, both for the irresponsible blessed and for the uptight unblessed. And when we are released, communication becomes possible.

Evangelism means that God can use one person to help another find freedom.

Think of the person in your life who has been most used of God to set you free from the areas that have blocked you as a person. It may not be the person who brought you to the Lord. Perhaps it is someone you met before or after that time; someone God used to release you from being just a giver or a receiver; just a talker or a doer.

If you are in Christ, you have been to some degree set free. You have been set free from certain things that bound you, set free to become a person who can be involved, can risk, can love deeply. You are in the process of moving from shackles toward the freedom to love and the freedom to fail.

Who was that person who came along? What did he do? What did he say? How did he listen? If we could find the key phrases that describe these people whom God has sent into our lives, we would have a more complete picture of what authentic New Testament evangelism looks like.

Unselfish . . . compassionate . . . honest . . . clinical . . . loving . . . patient. Such words describe the most effective evangelists, yet many of the books written about evangelism do not describe people like this.

Let us take heart. Ordinary people can become the true evangelists, the true communicators. Anyone who has been set free to be himself, to be vulnerable, to risk failure, to go the second mile—he belongs among the royal priesthood who are the thrust and hope and heartbeat of the emerging church.

Note: Portions of this article appeared in a slightly different form in FAITH AT WORK Magazine and in two books: *No Longer Strangers* by Bruce Larson, and *The Emerging Church* by Bruce Larson and Ralph Osborne, both published by Word, Inc., Waco, Texas. This material is used with the permission of the copyright holders.

Questions for Reflection

1. How is my world changing?
2. How am I changing?
3. What in society needs changing?
4. What is the Christian's role in a changing world?

2

Who Is the Man Outside Christianity?

By George Hunter III

Who is the man outside Christianity? When we are talking about "the outsider," who are we talking about? And, in general terms, what is the needed strategy for evangelizing the outsider today? Now this task of talking about the outsider is one that I approach with some humility. Even though I have thought and studied about this for a long time, I cannot pretend that I understand the outsider. I'm acutely aware of this because I met a fellow just a couple of weeks ago who actually pretends to understand his wife. And I thought to myself as soon as he said this, "What a presumptuous fool! By definition, no man understands his wife." I am saying this with tongue in cheek, but I am really making this point: if we do not *really* understand the other person that we are married to, then how much less likely it is that we understand a great host of people who have chosen, at least so far, not to contract themselves in another form of covenant to that one whom we call Lord.

I am hesitant also because this is a very difficult topic. Human beings simply do not fit into neat theoretical categories. Men differ from each other, and indeed, men differ within themselves at the various stages of life, in the various groups they live in, and in their changing moods. And let's face it, the social, political and economic currents that operate upon men and influence them and condition them are both massive and complex, and who among us can pretend to have his mind around all the great events and movements and influences of our time enough to critique and understand their impact upon human beings?

Then, there is of course no such animal as the "typical outsider," so that what I am talking about this afternoon is a generalization. But I would contend that we not only can, but must, generalize about this fellow called "the outsider" and we must do so just as accurately as we can. Because, part of our mission *is* to him, and we do not know how to conduct our mission most faithfully and most effectively unless we understand the soil in which we seek to plant the seed. Like it or not, most human beings today are outsiders.

Some 80 percent of the people of our globe are not professing Christians and when you face the stark fact that a great percentage of nominal Christians are functioning outsiders, whether or not they are technical outsiders, then we are talking about the men who basically represent our entire mission field with perhaps just a few quaint exceptions.

Coming to grips with the outsider is also an imperative because, let's face it, most evangelism movements and most evangelism programs do not take the outsider seriously and are not in fact designed for him. They are designed for the man who's already partly inside, who already has a Christian memory, and the man who already is at least connected with a Christian family, and perhaps attends church some. While we can consider him a functional outsider, he at least shares our thought-world and feels culturally identified with Christianity. The point is, most of our basic strategies and programs do not have the real outsider in conscious mind and purpose.

The other problem is that those evangelism movements and programs that do beam themselves to the outsider, do not in fact take him seriously. They speak to a phantom outsider *who does not exist,* or if he does, his numbers are diminishing. Most evangelism movements and programs and radio programs, for instance, that try to reach the outsider, generally presuppose things about the outsider that are not in fact true. Things like, he already accepts the authority of the Bible, or that he already understands our theological jargon, or that he conducts all of his life looking for the way to Heaven. But the outsider is *not* automatically tuned in on our wave length, and most evangelistic approaches pathetically presuppose that he is. So these are our imperatives, and acknowledging the difficulty of this task, and the church's present floundering, we must come to terms with this and begin to blaze some trails.

Let us talk about the outsider in three senses: in his relationship to the Christian message, in his relationship to the Christian church, and perhaps, somewhat presumptuously, in his relationship to the Christian God. What can we broadly generalize about him under these three categories?

First, his relationship to the Christian message. The general outsider is *not* some brilliant fire-breathing atheist or agnostic. Most outsiders are not, in fact, brilliant people who have studied the Christian faith and have perceived some intrinsic fallacies and have willingly, knowingly, and consciously rejected the Christian faith and its claim upon them. The outsider did not block out a point in his life and study the Bible, the ecumenical creeds, Calvin's Institutes, and the sermons of Tillich in order to get representative in-depth exposures to the Christian faith upon which he could then make a rational judgment. That just hasn't happened. Most outsiders are largely unconscious outsiders. They are the victims, or if you please, the recipients of influences and processes and other conditioning forces of which they are largely unconscious. For example, take the issue of a man's neighborhood environment. In Great Britain, Bishop E. R. Wickham wrote the book *Church and People in an Industrial City,* showing that in the suburbs of Great Britain 25 out of every 100 people are professing Christians and churchmen; but when you go into the inner city, the ghettos, only 3 percent of the people of Great Britain are professing Christians and churchmen. Twenty-five percent in the suburbs, 3 percent in the cities. Now what kind of conclusion do you draw from that? You either contend that God *likes* suburban people more than he likes ghetto people, which is dubious, or you face the brute fact that the social setting in which a man is placed may largely determine whether he finds plausible our message about a God of love and hope whom you can trust. There are other factors involved, but I am simply trying to stress that the forces that condition men qualify the degree to which they might be open to our message.

Talking about America, most Americans, and almost all outsiders, are very largely ignorant of the Christian message; or even worse, they may be misinformed about it. Back in 1950 George Gallup and his fellow travelers took a survey asking representative American people to "Name the four Gospels." He found that 35 percent could name all four, 4 percent could name three, 4 percent could name two of the gospels, 4 percent could name one—leaving 53 out of every 100 adult Americans who could not even name one of the four Gospels. I don't want to be presumptuous and read more into that data than is legitimate, but I would suggest that if a man cannot name the four Gospels, he is probably not intimately familiar with their content! We have a vast generation of biblical "ignostics" in our country and that is in fact the situation for evangelism today, and these percentages would presumably be higher for the outsider than they would be for the insider.

The outsider has a very limited knowledge of the Christian faith—what might be called a loose, randomized set of diluted images about Christianity. For instance, he knows something about Christmas but imaginally connected with his images about Christmas are his images about our American babyhood cult and the commercialism with which the Christian tradition has become saturated.

And there's Easter and he's exposed to Easter images, but also to images about spring flowers and the coming of springtime. He knows a few sayings from the biblical tradition. He knows about the Golden Rule, he knows about turn the other cheek, and a few things like that.

There are some anomalies in his mind. He's high on Jesus but if you ask him, "Who was Jesus? What did Jesus teach? What was Jesus like? What were his essential concerns?" very likely he will not be able to tell you. If you ask him, "Do you profess a religion?" he will likely say "Yes" and he may indeed say that his religion is the Sermon on the Mount, and yet he likely has not read the Sermon on the Mount at any time in recent memory. If you ask him "What is Christianity basically about and what do you understand a Christian to be?" what he will come up with is sheer moralism. You know, "A Christian is basically a nice person, a loyal citizen; it's a blending of white American middle-class morality with nationalism." And that, with perhaps the infusion of a few randomly extracted biblical texts, would pretty well wrap up his image of what a Christian is.

Let me stress some other things that I think can be said about the outsider and his relationship to the Christian message with at least high probability. For one, he has probably already rejected some versions of the Christian faith. He doesn't live in some kind of protected enclosure. He has had at certain points in his life some exposure to some brands of professing Christianity and generally speaking they have turned him off, and sometimes for quite understandable reasons that I would sympathize with in toto. Sometimes the only kind of religion that he has been exposed to is the "pie in the sky in the sweet by and by," or the kind of religion that is no more than sheer legalism, or moralism, or superpatriotism or self-righteousness.

Another thing we can say is that he very proudly rejects dogmatism, not only dogmatic attitudes but also the names that he would associate with dogmatism. He probably rejects, or at least is not acutely interested in, all theologians. He probably is not interested in what ecumenical councils have proclaimed and, if Lord Soper is correct, and I think he is, some outsiders are not especially interested in what the Bible has to say and, for all practical purposes, in talking to the outsider we have a radically reduced canon. The Old Testament is probably out, in our initial points of contact with him, and most of the New Testament as well. He's not interested, initially at least, in what Paul or John had to say because imaginally he associates those names with the kind of dogmatism he has rejected. But he *is* interested in Jesus and if you can talk to him about what Jesus has to say, then very likely you will find a point of contact within him.

Another thing we can say very briefly is that he finds the language in which the Christian message is usually couched to be a strange language of another era, a bygone day. As

Lawrence Lacour has frequently said, especially in relation to the outsider, "We must remit our language or we will short-change our hearers."

One other factor should be stressed about his relationship to the message: The outsider does not generally presuppose the relevance of the Christian faith for his life. Now that can sound like a platitude, and even a cliché, but let me say what I mean by it by way of some substance. The outsider does ask some very big questions and he is motivated by some great needs and desires and yearnings that, if not found in all men, are certainly found in most men. I have discovered through both reading and exposure to outsiders that questions like these are some of the questions that dominate their lives: How can I accept myself? How can I best relate to other people? How can I cope with loneliness, with boredom, with suffering? How can I choose my job? How can I raise my children to the greatest possible happiness? How can I find a purpose and a meaning for my life? How can I face the death of my loved ones? How can I face my own death? How can we face the future with security and hope? How can we bring about a just world and a world of peace and a world of equality?

Great numbers of outsiders are asking those questions. You say, "Well, those *are* the very questions that the Christian faith is directly related to." Yes, but the point is *he does not perceive that!* You ask him. He does not automatically assume the relevance of the Christian message for the deepest yearnings of his existence. Ask him and he will say Christian faith has little to do with his deepest legitimate concerns. "Christianity is just being a nice person, a good citizen, and obeying some superficial laws or rules. It's the kind of thing that is real swell for people who are 'that type' but 'it doesn't reach me at the gut level,' " he would exclaim. And so, this much at least, can be generalized about the outsider relationship to the Christian message.

Second, let me share some generalizations about his relationship to the Christian church. I think one thing we can say is that, very likely, he is even more estranged from the Christian church than he is from the Christian message. He is much more likely to consciously and overtly reject the Christian church than to reject the Christian message. Dr. Soper tells us in many of his writings that in his forty-three years of speaking in the open air on a week-by-week basis to outsiders in London, roughly one-half of all the questions and challenges that are hurled at him by outsiders have to do with the church, men's rejection of the church, man's antipathy toward the church.

I have worked through a lot of material trying to decide how to classify and categorize their perception of the church and their relationship to it. At least six categories are roughly suggested, and I'll say just a bit under each of these categories: the church's expertise, character, good will, prestige, dynamism and credibility.

 First, *expertise.* Once theology was the queen of the sciences. Today, no fool would pretend that she still enjoys that kind of status in the intellectual world. Practically speaking, great hosts of men today are not sure that Christians know what they are talking about, and compared to the scientists and other people who have very sophisticated and demonstrable disciplines, the outsider is not sure that Christian theologians and their poorer cousins, Christian parsons, even have a method for acquiring the truth about ultimate issues and man's existence.

Contrast, for instance, the theologian's image with that of the scientist. The scientist has a method that he can spell out in five or six understandable steps and he can state his hypothesis in advance. He then conducts his experiment and announces whether the hypothesis was verified, and he can replicate that experiment and its proof a thousand times. He has, at least in the popular mind, a demonstrable method for finding out what is true. The theologian today certainly has a great burden of proof to prove that he has any demonstrable expertise at all in the realms of the great issues.

Second, the field of *the churches' character.* Briefly put, Christians are not perceived as being good people, or as being any "gooder" than nonchurch people. One of the great controversies, of course, is over the question whether or not you can be just as good a person without going to church. And when you amplify this with the fact that the church at times has been brutally dishonest and corrupt, it's pretty hard to make a case to the outsider for the character of the church.

Third, is the category of *good will.* Outsiders are not convinced that the church is for folks like them. They believe that the church exists for its own folks, for the power structure, for the monied people, and the people of influence, for the people with fine clothes, the beautiful people, etc. They generally do not assume that the church stands as a beacon in their community, a beacon of good will for all the people.

Fourth is the gap at the point of *prestige.* This is related to some other categories, of course. The church and its ministers are not high in the popular status rating today compared to say science, medicine, government, education, and numbers of other institutions and their professionals.

Fifth is the point of *dynamism.* The church is not thought to be interesting, exciting, or even fashionable. Compared to a number of other things like television, entertainment, sports, science and politics, the church, they say, is not where it's happening. The church is not where the action is, or as some of our young people put it, "Fellow, the church doesn't turn me on." There's the gap at the point of dynamism.

Last, the point of *credibility.* They doubt whether the church and its people really believe and live by the Christian gospel in so far as they are able to dimly understand that gospel. They see in the church the same self-seeking, the same politicking, the same success patterns, and the same success motives, that most other men and institutions more or less live by, are motivated by, and make decisions upon. They see the church whitewashing unjust wars. They see the church smoke-screening racial discrimination and segregation and some of the other obvious evils that a common man knows in his very bones, though he may not be able to articulate it, are unjust and that a credible church would renounce it and seek to redeem it.

You would be surprised how many men, how many outsiders know—where Methodism is strong—that Methodist ministers are moved and advanced on the basis of how much money they raised in the current pastorate, how many buildings they have built, and how many members they have recruited. They know that the institutional church in our time has been captured by a cash register culture; this is their perception, although we inside the church could give many qualifiers. In their perception they do not see the church as being a credible institution. They look at our grassroots positions on war and other issues and say, "Well, I don't know much about Jesus, but I doubt that this church is what he had in mind."

And especially scandalous are our organic divisions in the church. Think about it. We announce to the world a gospel of reconciliation and we try to announce that good news out of a divided church. They look at us and they say, "Well, it would be great if your message of reconciliation was true, but you yourselves are not reconciled. I suppose we'll have to graze in greener pastures." And that is in fact the case.

Then third, let me attempt something about the outsider's relation to our God. And here I may seem even more presumptuous because I will be the first to admit that neither I nor you can stand in another human being's skin and ultimately know what kind of relationship with the Christian God he has. And I for one would never renounce the possibility that God can relate to human beings in ways that extend far past my abilities to comprehend his relation—creating activity.

Let me share one example that comes from a good friend of mine, Ed Beck. Back in 1960, he was the captain of a preaching basketball team that toured the Orient. When they got there, one of the things they asked the missionaries was, "Are there any sections where the gospel has never been preached?" The missionaries said, "Well, we know of several villages where, as far as we know, no missionary has ever spoken. Why don't we take you to one of those?" So they went to a particular village, which was a unique village in many ways. For several generations, this village had never made any warfare against other villages. They held all things in common. There were no class distinctions there. The old and the young and those who could not work were taken care of. There was no crime. It was a miniature paradise, in these and other ways. This basketball team with Ed Beck went in and preached the good news of Christ and afterwards the chieftain, or whatever the head man was called, rushed up and through the interpreter said this to Ed: "Thank you for telling us about Jesus. You must know that we have known him now for over a hundred years, but until today we have never known his name." You see, the spirit of Jesus Christ is alive and loose in the world, working in ways that, frankly, extend far beyond our comprehension. Of course, many other examples could be given.

Let me shift categories at this point and talk about *"the secular man,"* not just the outsider. We know that when we talk about the outsider, we are usually talking about the secular man, and of course, many times when we talk about the insider we are talking about the secular man as well.

Let me make just three or four suggestions about the outsider and God in this way. First, from the German theologian and martyr, Dietrich Bonhoeffer, we get this insight: most men are becoming secularized in a sense that they use GOD less and less for help and answers. Bonhoeffer made the incisive perception that most men in their religion, loosely speaking, have really used God in two ways. They have used him to get help when they could not help themselves, and they used him to provide an answer when they could not answer some mystery in other terms. Through science man is now able to help himself more and more and answer questions more and more. Therefore, men have to call on God, in this sense, less and less. One statement we can make is that the outsider, in so far as he is a secular man, is a man that through his history calls on God for help and answers less and less. David Edwards of Cambridge elucidates this. He says, "When modern people feel sick, they want medicine. When their crops are poor, they want fertilizers. When they are ignorant, they want education. When their relationships are entangled, they know that they ought to profit by a cool, scientific study of the underlying economic or emotional problems, and when they want rain, they do not beat on drums." We are witnessing the pushing to the perimeter of life the approach to God that Bonhoeffer called "the deus ex machine," the stopgap God.

The second generalization: men, in so far as they are secular, and this would include most outsiders, are more inclined as Colin Williams put it—"to live from below rather than from above." More and more, they live in terms of this world. More and more they live their lives and make their decisions without conscious reference to the traditions of the Christian church or some supramundane authority, including God. Indeed, most men cope fairly well most of the time without calling on God, which is, of course, part of our problem.

The third and last thing I want to say is a bit complex in stating. Because of the secularization process, man's awareness of the transcendent realm is diminished, and what remains lacks moral authority. Let me restate it. The secular man's awareness of transcendence, of the ultimate, of mystery, of the beyond in the midst of our lives is diminished, reduced, diluted, and lacks moral authority.

I do not say that man's awareness of the beyond has become erased or obliterated, as some very foolish secularization theorists have contended. You can look all around you and see that men are groping for ultimate reality in many ways.

We are told, and I think rightly, that a motive, the dominant motive perhaps, behind the drug culture, is the quest for mystical experience. We are told that all over the world, including America and Great Britain, there is a revival of belief in luck and in superstition. And astrology, of all things, is enjoying a stampeding revival. Other expressions of religious quest include the isms of the twentieth century: imperialism, communism, capitalism, nationalism, militarism, Fascism, and Nazism. Two presuppositions that are ultimately religious stand behind each of these "isms." One: "God is on our side"; even the secularized Marxist version says "the inevitable force of history is behind us and is on our side." Second, their cause is raised to the status of a holy cause; the enemy is totally depraved; the "ism" demands devout commitment from its followers.

In the broad sense, religion is rampant in our time, but man's awareness of transcendence, at least generally, *is* diminished, less strong than it used to be, and it lacks moral authority. For instance, a few years ago in Great Britain, a Gallup survey was made asking people, "Do you believe in God?" Eighty percent of the people said "Yes" and the other

twenty percent checked either "No" or "Uncertain." Of the
eighty percent who checked "Yes" they then asked the question, "Does your belief in God make any demands on you?"
Two-thirds of the eighty percent said "No."

You see, man's awareness of the ultimate is reduced, diminished. It's something that he still wonders about, and he
tries to use sometimes and wants on his side, but he does not
recognize that beyond the realm of the temporal, there is a
Personality who is his Lord, and who has a claim upon him.

Now let me risk the hazardous vocation of suggesting some
general imperatives for evangelizing the outsider today. Some
imperatives have already been implied and there's no need
to be redundant, but several merit underscoring or extension.

First, *we simply must saturate our culture with the Christian message.* We must pull out all the stops to acquaint men
with our gospel. This is a massive undertaking, because men
are not only uninformed but misinformed. We simply must
do all within our power to bring all men to the kind of suffi-
cient basic grasp of what our faith is about that will enable
them to deeply sense whether this faith warrants their commitment and their lives.

Yes, this does mean the use of mass media—but not necessarily an overreliance upon expensive television. Many of us
are convinced that television is *not* the most effective medium
for teaching post-Sesame Street folks, and certainly not in
comparison to the cost. I would risk the hypothesis that there
are two media that have far more potential than we might
realize. One is radio. More people own more radios and listen
to more radio programming more hours per day than ever
before; and radio programming is an awesome shaper of as-
sumptions and attitudes in the popular mind. So far, mainline
Christianity has largely neglected radio exposure, naively
turning it over to hacks and charlatans. The other potential
medium worth great investment is the pamphlet. Our culture
is ripe for a renaissance in pamphleteering; tens of millions
of people desperately want to read but lack the time to wade
through tomes. Notice how in the day of a publications explosion, it is the very brief novel, *Love Story,* that causes a
stampede. It goes without saying that the format for radio

and pamphlet must be so new and intriguing as to suggest instant contemporaneity, and the language must be noneclesiastical, secular language. Anything smacking of "sermonette" will be instantly rejected by our target auditor—and I don't blame him.

Second, *we must take appropriate steps to enable the outsider to perceive the church differently.* This doesn't mean just polishing up our "image"; it means a new reformation of the church in our time. Because, while you and I know enough of the church we love to qualify their indictments, there is nevertheless much truth in them. By and large church services *are* dull; the church *is* self-interested; and many professing Christians and churches *do* not in fact take the way of Jesus Christ seriously. When the church deeply loves and serves men and lives by the message she proclaims, then some of those people the cause can use most will joyfully return to the community of faith.

Third, I suspect *we must much more widely employ the small group meeting* to bring outsiders at least to the fringe of involvement; I think we are foreseeing the second coming of the "house church" in great numbers. Many people, especially from the lower classes, may not come to a church building where they'd feel conspicuous and out of place; but they just might come by invitation to a group meeting where people accept each other, and share, and laugh together, and explore, and affirm what they can with integrity.

Last, we must find ways to demonstrate the profound relevance of our faith to the needs men have—individually and corporately. You'd expect me to restress this, because I see that as the major problem in the relationship between the typical outsider and the Christian message. When we can demonstrate what we sing—that "The hopes and fears of all the years are met in him tonight"—then great numbers will give our message a second chance. For some, the fresh exposure to this most relevant of all messages will be self-commending and they will choose to venture that great transition into the Christian life and mission.

Questions for Reflection

1. What is the essential content of the Christian message?
2. What is the relationship between the Christian message and the Christian messenger in terms of personal morality, social concern, and personal witness?
3. How can my local church identify and minister to the "man outside Christianity" in my community?

3

What I Have Learned About Communicating With the Outsider

By Lord Donald Soper

The problem with the outsider has to be subdivided because many of those who are outsiders once belonged to a Christian faith and are insiders in respect of many other of the associations to which modern man is committed. On the other hand, many of those who are outsiders from the standpoint of the Christian faith are also victims of the prevalent sense of alienation in which they *feel* they are outsiders.

I would like to make some comment about those in the first place who are outsiders in respect of the Christian organizations and what problematically we have to face and practically what we can do, and to present some kind of treatment for the other two sorts and categories of people to which I have adverted—the insider in the secular world who is the outsider from the Christian faith and organization standpoint, and the outsider per se.

Now when I was a boy in England most people who did not go to church at least knew the name of the church they stayed away from. There was a loose connection and the habits of the church were not entirely remote from the conduct and practice of those who perhaps infrequently darkened the doors of the sanctuary—they were still the residual legatees of the kind of traditions which belonged to the non-conformist tradition. I wonder how many of you experienced, enjoyed, or suffered the kind of Sunday which was de rigeur in our family.

We rose somewhat later than on weekdays and after our breakfast we went to morning Sunday school. After morning Sunday school we stayed on for morning church. After church we came home and discussed the sermon and had lunch. After lunch we went back to Sunday school in the afternoon. Thereafter, we repaired home for high tea for which we sang grace. We only said it during the week, but high tea with shrimp seemed to us an occasion for the singing of grace and it was always sung on Sunday! After the singing of grace and the consumption of high tea we repaired to the drawing room where my mother played the piano and we sang hymns until it was time to go to church again. We went to church in the evening, came home, and had supper. Whereafter my father said, "It is a good thing to go to bed early on Sunday"—a magnificent illustration of making a virtue out of a necessity. We were played out, we were done for! And if we had stayed up it would have been more hymns; and therefore we went to church most of Sunday and went to bed early.

Now when I recite this to my grandchildren they say "poor grandpa." But I really don't want their sympathy. I only want the simple recognition that that kind of churchmanship has gone and it will not return. It will not return for a variety of reasons—some good and some bad. I will not weary you with them. I merely make a comment that the whole habit of a specialized religious institution which is particular to the conduct of Sunday has already been eroded to such an extent that many of you do not regard the extension of religious exercises to go beyond 12:00 noon on Sunday. And furthermore there is a progressive movement away from the kind of regularized Sabbatarianism.

Now those who are outside the particular form of religious exercise would not fifty years ago have necessarily been outside the other ministries of the church. But I expect for some of you the practice of Sunday observance was a part of the practice of family prayers, and of religious exercises during the week in the general setting of a religious framework which was associated with the church to which people belonged. It is true that in the Rhondda Valley and in the Welsh valleys generally the church was not only the place to which people

repaired for spiritual worth; it was also the sum total of the
society in which those people lived. And those in the political
movement of my day who are perhaps the most remote from
the exercises of Christian piety, learned how to speak in the
church, practiced their first educational exercises in the
church, found their wives or their husbands in the church.
For them the church was the center of their social life. Now
we are in an age in which secularism means that none of
those things now prevail to the extent to which once they did,
—at any rate in the country from which I come. I shall not
be presumptuous enough to speak of what happens here. You
will draw your own conclusions and make your own compari-
sons.

Now what are we to do? Are we to assume that we are on
the verge, perhaps, if we can find the right evangelist or the
right gimmick, of some kind of return to that kind of churchmanship? I should have supposed that the motor car, the TV
set, and the increased mobility of the modern community has
rendered this as a waste of time as a recognizable project; and
I would invite you to believe that our attitude to the outsider
in this particular respect must be that we have to form appropriate measures of churchmanship which are not linked to
the pattern and to the precision of that world which has
passed away taking with it the good thing and some of those
things which were not so good. As my ultimate utterance before I repair back to England, I would presume to make one
comment: That within the framework of weekday activity
there is likely to be a compensation for an irrevocable loss of
the general fabric of Sunday observance in the old-fashioned
and somewhat totalitarian way in which it was the focus of
Christian discipleship.

Now a second point: We must be careful to recognize that
those who are outsiders from the standpoint of organized
Christianity are, many of them, insiders in other human relationships and intellectual connotations. For example, I refer
to the Rhondda Valley, the Welsh valleys, the mining valleys.
What has taken the place of the church in the mining valley?
Now, the working man's club, or the local football team, or the
administrations of the local governments in their wisdom have

provided amenities, cultural and otherwise, which were the
monopoly of the church in past generations.

And it is the business of an educated and consistent Christianity today to minister within the fabric of the society where
so many of our contemporaries are in fact, insiders. The value
of the work that I try to do in Hyde Park is not necessarily
a fully evangelical task, fully evangelically fulfilled—of course
it isn't. We have no hymns, we suffer from the lack of any
ability to take a collection; and we are not in any sense the
same thing as a church service, but we are in touch with those
people for whom Hyde Park on Sunday afternoon is the modern equivalent of the kind of social gathering that once was
confined to the church. And that's where we've got to be. I
don't go to Hyde Park on Sunday afternoon just for the plea-
sure of hearing my own voice or for any false exhibitionism.
I go there because if people won't come to us where we are,
we must go to them where they are. And the ministry of
interpenetration of those who are outside the church, but
inside many of the organizations of our modern life, is an
imperative ministry. I will permit myself two comments on it.

The first is that we must prevent ourselves from having
any sense that we are undertaking a lesser spiritual vocation.
If we have to limit our spiritual exercises and if we have to
tailor that ministry within the necessary framework of a secular organization, I say that three quarters of an hour on Sunday afternoon in badinage and fruitless argument and friendly
or unfriendly controversy for the sake of being able to put in
a word of the gospel in perhaps five minutes, then is not only
permissible, but acceptable. What do you know of the organizations within the area in which you minister—the secular organizations? And I am not particularly talking of the service
clubs—which seem to me very often to be religion with its
backbone extricated. I am not talking about those who are
afraid or unprepared to take the theological propositions of
the Christian faith seriously and therefore have to indulge in
a less rigorous kind of social environment. I'm talking about
the trade unions; I'm talking about the various secular organizations; and I'm presuming to say that inasmuch as this is
where things happen, this is where the Christian church has

to be. But it's no good going in unless you have some kind of expertise. It's no good going in with the platitudes which may stand a fair chance of being acceptable in a fairly comatose sermon, but would be thoroughly unacceptable within the framework of these societies today that have grown up to take the place of what once was a monopoly exercised by the Christian church.

But I would like to add one further thing before I sit down: And it has to do with the outsider per se. The most clamant and the most pertinent indictment of what we are pleased to call modern society in the west, and indeed this covers the whole spectrum of modern society, is what our friends of the left call "alienation." Man does not belong anywhere anymore. He has become alienated from the soil. He has become alienated from the normal rhythms of life. That is to say, he manufactures his light and he is indifferent to the seasons. He lives in the vast cohabitations of cities. And as Ted Wickham so pertinently says, "There is no more lethal foe of natural religion than the artificiality of industrialized civilization." He lives in high rise flats where he can completely forget not only the time of day, but all the natural systems that may persist in superstition among those who live in the countryside but nevertheless are constant reminders that life is richer than thought and indeed more mysterious than electricity. And this is one of the ways in which man today has become alienated in the sense that he no longer belongs. He is an outsider. He has manufactured gadgets to take the place of the natural sequences of life which God ever intended to be promptings and suggestions of immortality. But even more important he is alienated because he feels no lot or part in the actual conduct of affairs.

He feels that events happen in the giant mood of indifferent malaise rather than in the consequential behavior of individuals. We have noticed in contemporary democratic affairs in Great Britain how alienated many have become when they feel that ultimately their own destinies in our country are decided in the Pentagon over here rather than in the deliberations of Westminster at home. And how indeed the effectiveness of any one individual is minimized by the fact that he is an isolated creature in a world in which community has given place to amenity. I mean by that that the vast areas that I know in London, and I dare say you know in the great cities of this country, have become denaturalized so that there is no sense of community even at the level of tittle-tattle. There is no sense of community even at the level of being thrown too close together. There is no center to the life which people live. This is the supreme problem of the outsider.

I believe that to overcome this problem of the outsider we have radically to reassess our whole concept of what the kingdom of God is all about. I believe the kingdom of God is about that kind of society in which people are not outsiders whether their skin is black, whether their means are few; or whether they are literate or illiterate, whether they belong to the favored continents, whether they belong to the "haves" or the "have-nots." Until we can create a sense of the over-arching love of God for them all, until we can create the economic and social environment in which they all will find a suitable opportunity of full development, they will remain out-siders, for so many of them have at long last perceived that fault which lies at the root of so much contemporary religion. That is, that so much contemporary religion is class-ridden, is committed to certain groups and as an overall commitment of God's love for all mankind has manifestly failed to justify its claims.

I would make this final comment. It is increasingly evident that the proper way for the Christian church to go forward is to embrace the truly revolutionary concept for which Jesus lived and for which he died and for which he rose again; that is to say that outside the love of God we are indeed, all of us, in an alien land, but within the love of God, we are all in a homeland and we must all be gathered at the same hearth fire.

Questions and Answers

Q. If a man in Great Britain professed the Christian ethic, but did not attach it to the Christian religion, what would be your attitude to him?

A. My attitude would be in strict concert with the teaching of our Lord, "He that is not against us is for us." He who gives a cup of cold water in the name of a disciple—not in the name of the Lord, but in the name of a disciple—his reward is certain. I am sick to death of people saying you can't be a Christian unless you recite the right words at the right time with a suitably demure expression that you understand them fully. I believe the essential Christian forward movement is to welcome everybody in the spirit of John Wesley by saying, "If your heart is with me, give me your hand."

The fact is that we are in a post-Christian age. And when for instance people like Bertrand Russell used to deny Christian verities, they were using Christian standards by which to do it. Now I would not be content for the man who said, "Now let's have the brotherhood of man, but not talk about the fatherhood of God," because I should have to point out to him that you never know that the other man is your brother until you first ascertain that you both belong to the same father. And therefore the process of Christian morality ultimately depends on Christian theology. And I am most aware of this in the sense that unless we can conjoin our moral incentives to a decent theological background, some of those moral incentives will be insufficient. And that is why it is desperately important that those who practice the ethic of the Christian faith should be constantly reinforced by its power and its spirit because otherwise, sooner or later, they will find a dereliction of power and a loss of energy.

Q. What about "God talk"?

A. Well, my problem of course as an Englishman is that nothing divides us so much from you as our common language! I remember some years ago I hadn't been too long with contemporary theology over here, I landed on your shores and was immediately accosted by a reporter who said to me: "Is God dead?" I said I hadn't known he was unwell! And this piece of healthy blasphemy haunted me all the time that I was here. I don't know what you mean by "God talk." Is it that people object to the categories and the formularies which we use? Words like salvation, redemption? In the preliminary stages of evangelism none of them are of the slightest use. Not the slightest. They are overloaded with all kinds of complicated theories, they cannot be explained except in terms of divisive theologies and the first requirement in evangelism is not to prescribe for a man a series of dogmas to which he is to affix his heart and hand, but to bring him into personal touch with the living character of Jesus Christ, for it is the man who does the will who knows of the gospel. And it is only in the personal discipleship of Jesus Christ that we have any right to formalize our more careful metaphysical dogmas. Oh yes, it's a waste of time. It is a waste of time to quote the Bible to a man in the street, quite a waste of time. You can use the Bible of course to reinforce what you are saying. You can surprise him by telling him how expert are some of the words in the Bible to describe his own condition, but it is a sheer waste of time to sling a text at him as though that will prove anything.

Q. Do you see any great spiritual movement in England?

A. No, none at all. That is to say one would be very foolish to put any limits on the power of God. One would be very foolish to invest one's cassock with the authority of a prophetic cloak. I don't know what's going to happen, but if we are to make any observations and assessments based on evidence, the evidence that can be ascertained, I think the process away from the church is accelerating. And it may be that we are in for a period of darkness or at any rate, muted illumination. Whatever happens, I do not find myself in any mood of despair because the one thing that has comforted and assured me is that if Christianity has tended to seep out of organized religion, it is tending in the country I come from to seep into public government. And quite the most Christian thing that has happened in my lifetime is the welfare state. I began as a minister in a church on Old Kent Road, a dreary, sleazy part of London. And I have noted with gratification and thanks to God the way in which the old and dreadful sores of industrial poverty have no longer their septic and terrible impact upon the community in which we live. There are plenty of people who are still poor but there is an expression of Christian care which has never previously appeared; and when our Russian friends (and I was in Russia in August) still assume that we are living in Dickensian times, that is the supreme ultimatum for the rejection of their ideology.

Q. What about the state of the worker-priest movement?

A. The worker-priest movement in France has gone through three stages. First of all there are no worker-priests left in France. There are priests in industry. The reason for the change, which was initiated, I think, by the Archbishop of France, was that there was a basic fault in the concept of the worker-priest. Two basic faults, rather. One was that he was never completely assimilable within the worker framework for the precise reason that he was of a different intellectual caliber and therefore, however much he wished to integrate with the worker at the bench beside him, he was in fact already in a condition of cultural disparity. And the second was that if the worker on the bench beside him lost his job, he was out of work, but if the worker-priest lost his job, he was still a priest, and for these reasons among others the archbishops of France and then of Paris and finally by general decree the worker-priest movement was shut down and in its place was something which approximates far more the concept of the chaplain in the framework of industry. This has been partially effective. But here again one of the clauses of this particular assignment which is most dangerous is that when a denominational candidate of, say the Methodists, seeks office or seeks a position as chaplain within the works, then immediately the local Anglican parson may well feel that he ought to be there and the Catholic will assume automatically that he ought to be there and then the communist will want to be there too, and it produces, shall we say, a congestion at the tea break interval! I have always resisted the idea that there is a working class creature who is radically different from the rest of the community. It might have been true, I think it was, in the early days of the industrial revolution because I think you know far better than we do that the so-called difference between the white and blue-collared worker has almost totally disappeared. And you have gone further than we have. Workers in the country from which I come, that is to say working people, still wear cloth caps and chokers and speak with a manifest accent which is distinguishable from that which is pseudo-Oxford. In your country I wouldn't presume to know too intimately what goes on, but it seems to me that you have broken down some of these class distinctions that are represented sartorially and therefore it is a great mistake when the church attempts to segregate men from one another even in its ministries. I have a hearty dislike for those who say we must have "a young man's preacher," or "an old man's preacher," or we must cosset this or that particular group. There is one gospel and unless we can present it comprehensively we had better shut up shop.

Q. How can we as ministers get out into this everyday week?
A. Let me make this suggestion. Have you tried open-air preaching? Now don't be cross with me if I say this to you. So many people assume that they go out two Sunday afternoons to a particular spot and if nobody comes they have exhausted the possibilities of open-air speaking in that area. It was the immortal William Booth of the Salvation Army who said that the Salvationists should go to that street corner and there they should stand and address the crowds and if after a year of regular meetings at that street corner nobody came, they should feel it then justifiable to move around to the next street! Now that may be an extravagance but it is worth remembering.

The other point is that people say, "If we are going to have an open-air meeting, let's find a nice open space," which is the last thing you want. It is likely to remain open space! What you want is a nice congested space. The best kind of open-air speaking can be done where the policeman is about to move you off.

I was in Washington Square some little while ago and thought we might have an open-air meeting. It was a marvelous place for an open-air meeting and I was with some friends of mine, some of your own ministers. In the center of the square there were quite a number of people hanging around and I thought I had better consult with a couple of cops who were there as to whether it was permissible and so I said, "Can we hold an open-air meeting?" and he said, "What for?" and I said, "To proclaim the Christian faith." He said he didn't know about that, "but I'll go and find out." So he and his friend went to find out and while they were away we had the meeting! Now you haven't heard of any repercussions have you? But now a little sanctified audacity in this field isn't a bad thing.

I can only suggest to you that it is a most exhilarating and rewarding exercise.

One of the reasons why people don't watch open-air speakers is that they have a healthy desire not to watch other people suffer. And it is always a bad thing if you are in pain when you are speaking in the open air or you give the impression that you are in pain. You must really give the impression that you are enjoying it. Some of you who have been to Hyde Park will, I think, bear me out that these are rambunctious occasions but it is supremely enjoyable. Now I say it's enjoyable. I have been knocked down a number of times, quite often by an inebriated Irishman. And I was knocked down frequently during the war when they objected to my pacifism which was not, shall we say, easily understood. But it is at least a glorious opportunity to speak to the outsider when it is very often denied to us by any other means we seek to attract him indoors.

The other way, of course, is the way of the social commitment. I am responsible for about thirteen hostels of various kinds in which we are involved with girls on probation, pregnant girls and unmarried mothers, and old people and alcoholics, and we find the local authorities most happy to cooperate with us to do jobs they know full well they can't do themselves. But here again please acquit me of any attempt to come over on a brief visit and tell you what's what. I don't know. I only know what I have been able to attempt in the country from which I come, and I only know this, I wish to God that more and more parsons in England would make the same experiment and that they might do it a lot better than I have done.

Q. When you are speaking to the outsider, and you begin not with something you would understand to be central to the faith but rather, initiatory, what are some of the things that you talk about that engage the sustained attention of the outsider?

A. If I am talking to a crowd in Hyde Park, as I shall be on Sunday, I shall take the precaution of reading the Sunday paper before I get there. I know quite well that some issues will be dominant in the minds of those who will be there. Dominant though not of supreme import. I can give you an illustration: When I was in Hyde Park last Sunday, we were faced with the prospect that in the New Year there would be an industrial relations bill which, in our own terminology, was going to "clobber the union." Now this had front page publicity in the morning paper—the Sunday paper—so I talked about it. This is the important thing—to begin where people are and not where you would like them to be. And it doesn't matter where you begin. There is nothing in this world which cannot be related to the gospel. I don't care a fig what it is about. If it's abortion, pornography . . . now I don't speak about sexual matters with an avidity because you can double your crowd, increase the attention, and decrease anything else! You can create far more heat than light . . . but at the same time the expertise of the open-air speaker is to take the question and make use of it. Whatever the question is, however frivolous or completely blasphemous, you've got to accept it. I mean, one of the questions that I remember being asked was, "Who washed up after the Last Supper?" Now my first reaction was one of shock. Then my second reaction was, "Here was a glorious opportunity to talk about the Last Supper," which I did. There are very few questions which, however superficial and peripheral, cannot be related to the gospel in its ultimate sense. And the business of the open air speaker is to start there. If, for instance, I were to get up on Sunday next and say "I want you all to sign the pledge because alcohol is the devil in solution and it's pernicious anyhow," the crowd would disperse. But if a man in the crowd says, "Why don't you talk about alcoholism?" or "What's the point, why can't I drink my beer if I want to?" and I answer him, I say the same thing. The psychological impact of answering a question which is real to him makes all the difference to its acceptability with the rest of the crowd!

Another very important point is: Don't tell funny stories. If you make a joke, throw it away. If anyone wants to pick it up, they are welcome to it but don't wait for it. There is nothing more disastrous than waiting for the guffaw that doesn't happen.

You can be hard hitting as you like, but get interested in what you say, have a suitable vocabulary so that you don't have to repeat your words too frequently, and communicate to the crowd, if you can, or to the people to whom you minister that, for you, the Christian adventure is an exciting enterprise as well as a solemn one. But it is one which commands the most widespread reflection on your part on all issues which are real to other people and I believe it cannot but bear fruit. However, as I say, there is nothing further from my intention than to carry coals to Newcastle or teach my grandmother to suck eggs.

Questions for Reflection

1. How do I presently relate to "outsiders" in both secular and religious settings?
2. What strategies might I employ to better express my concern for "outsiders"?
3. How can my local church become more inclusive of all persons regardless of their economic or racial status?

4

Call to Cooperative Churchmanship

By George Outen

I appeal to you, brethren, by the name of our Lord Jesus Christ, that all of you agree that there be no dissensions among you, but that you be united in the same mind and the same judgment. For it has been reported to me by Chloe's people that there is quarreling among you, my brethren. What I mean is that each one of you says, "I belong to Paul," or "I belong to Apollos," or "I belong to Cephas," or "I belong to Christ." Is Christ divided?—1 Corinthians 1:10-13a   (RSV)

"Surely Christ has not been divided among you." I am afraid that one of Paul's greatest fears has become a reality. Christ has been divided into major denominations and numerous sects. Historically, Christians have made war against other Christians in the name of Christ and for his sake! Today we would not wage conflict on a battlefield, but we vie against one another nonetheless—all in the spirit of Christ—you understand. Indeed, the irony is that I feel the need to begin this discussion, not by relating ways in which churches may cooperate, but by justifying the need for such ecumenical ventures.

There comes to mind almost immediately two occasions and examples of cooperation between churches of differing persuasions. There are times when we worship together, but these are infrequent, and the reasons for such ventures may indeed be suspect. Often a Good Friday service, an Easter sunrise service, or a Thanksgiving Day service is the product of several denominations working together. A time of crisis such as occurred at the assassination of President Kennedy may also produce community-type worship opportunities. In fact this latter example may prove to be more legitimate than our high festival day endeavors. I suspect that the reason we join with fellow Christians at Thanksgiving or on Good Friday may be our need to avoid the embarrassment that comes from a half empty church on such an auspicious occasion. It is easy to "get together" when we are ashamed to face the apathy of our people alone. At such times the community-type service will at least fill one church and make our Thanksgiving Day celebration respectable in spite of the football game that lures most of our people away from the house of worship. If enough churches cooperate we may succeed in camouflaging a deeper problem.

The second example of cooperation is likened to our interpretation of the first. Churches share together in programming when there is no alternative open but to cooperate or to die. In our large cities, for example, it sometimes becomes imperative that churches merge their Sunday schools, or youth programs, or jointly attack a problem that faces the community. To do otherwise would be impossible in the face of shrinking attendance coupled with rising costs. Or, in the latter case, our singular effort would raise the ire of the persons of the neighborhood who have come to see the utter necessity for a unified front in dealing with a common concern.

Moreover, within a given denomination as well as between different groups, churches suffering a serious decline in membership are willing to merge in order to pump life into what would otherwise soon be a corpse. In cities and in rural areas two or more dying congregations can thus lean upon one another and are propped up by such mergers while their demise is stayed, if only for a short time.

In such cases, death is only delayed if the root causes for the illness that prompted the merger are not diagnosed and corrected. In any case, cooperation is the result of sheer necessity and outward circumstances. It is the last resort of an institution about to face extinction.

If either of the pictures painted here is at all true, it is easy to see why Christ is divided. As long as our church is full on Thanksgiving Day, why join in with anyone else? If our local situation seems healthy and strong, why should we investigate the possibilities of shared experiences with the church across the street. When ecumenism or cooperation is seen as only the means to prevent embarrassment, or prolong the life of the dying, then it is to be expected that division will continue, even increase, for those who champion cooperative experiences for the wrong reasons also hurt the cause. My point is that those who join with fellow Christians in order to avoid embarrassment, and to feed upon one another in order that death may be avoided are doing so usually for the wrong reasons. Cooperation between Christian churches ought to emanate from positions of strength and not from the dregs of weakness. It is at this point I suppose that I must demonstrate why strong churches ought to seek to cooperate with other churches.

Quite often when we talk about cooperation we come at it from the wrong angle altogether. Therefore, I want to begin by approaching the rationale, the *raison d'être* for cooperation or ecumenism from the point of view of what is the mission of the church. When we begin asking the question, "Why does the church exist?" it is inevitable that we begin relating the church to the world. Paul Stagg in his book, *The Converted Church*,[1] says that in establishing an authentic style of evangelism for the recovery of biblical insights and the development of new approaches for our modern technological society the first question to raise is not, "What is the mission of the church?" This is a secondary question dependent upon an answer to a prior question which is, "What is God's mission in the world?" Only when we know what God is doing on earth can we know what we are called to do. If the church is called upon to participate in God's mission in the world then we must ask, "What is God's mission in the world?"—"What is he doing which involves us and to which we are called to be witnesses?"

At least one of the things that God is doing, according to the biblical witness, especially in the New Testament, is breaking down barriers that do not need to exist between man and

God, between man and man, and between man and himself. That there is to be a oneness in Christ is an essential theme of the New Testament. The thrust of the message is that there should be no barriers which keep men apart when there ought to be an active and realistic interchange in the community. Therefore, the church cannot afford to be involved in any kind of structures or any kind of stance which gets in the way of what God is trying to do in the world. If God is trying to get us together we had better not be caught in the position of keeping men apart. This is especially true if one of the significant parts of the mission of Jesus the Christ was to effect reconciliation among all men. It is an ironic contradiction if the very means ordained by God to facilitate cooperation among peoples is itself used to keep us at odds with one another. This is not a plea for organic union or merger, but simply a hope that there will be realistic and viable cooperation among the people of God.

Paul claims that God was in Christ reconciling the world to himself. He makes the further affirmation that this ministry of the reconciliation has now been given to us, the Christian church—the legacy of Christ. It is our job to do all we can to effect reconciliation between men. A good place to begin is by demonstrating how "all things cohere in Christ." Congregations that are strong in the faith need to lead the way in showing that in Christ, real unity of purpose and polity can be achieved.

Another reason for cooperative endeavors between strong and vibrant congregations is the need for the sharing of ideas and attitudes between persons on a meaningful and rather profound level. The church can provide an arena in which persons of varying backgrounds and persuasions can engage in the kinds of discussions that will promote new appreciation for other people. Is there a more essential need in our world today than the need for encouraging conversation and understanding between the people that make up the various segments of our society? In this important area the church could lead the way toward reconciliation. The need is so critical that any movement in this direction, even though small, is to be encouraged. The larger and stronger the churches involved the more effective might be any attempts at working together to implement a program or engage in relevant dialogue.

Whatever other failings there have been in the past in co-operative church work, one of the most glaring has been the lack of lay involvement in the formulation of the plans. Most often the ideas and strategies for ecumenical ventures have been confined to discussions between the clergy, professional type church workers, and perhaps a few lay leaders of the churches involved. Sometimes the fact that the pastors of several congregations are willing to meet on a regular, or even irregular, basis is construed as substantial evidence of significant cooperation. In some instances, where real antagonism and conflict between congregations have existed, such clergy meetings may be the splendid breakthrough needed to restore a spirit of brotherhood, but usually, they fall far short of any much needed adventure. Somehow, the laity must be shown the need for cooperation, encouraged to suggest ways in which this kind of engagement can be accomplished, and enabled to implement the projected plans. Real ecumenism takes place more often when the laity operate on all three levels and are not simply accessories after the fact. It misses the mark when laymen are asked to join in a "community" Thanksgiving Day service, "because it would be a nice thing to do." They must know the theological as well as the practical reasons for such a move. And as much as feasible, they should share in the formulation of the plans for that service.

Members of various congregations normally are in contact with one another in the business and professional world, at school and in community organizations. In those settings they discuss common problems and mutual concerns. However, it is often a different and a quite meaningful experience for those persons to meet as churchmen to discuss a projected joint venture. To deal with one's religious affiliation and to discuss theological reasons for cooperation will often elicit deep feeling tones and cause the group to interact at a more personal level than does the business or community setting. How then can churches begin to move toward each other in response to the call to cooperative churchmanship?

In his book, *The Church Reclaims the City*,[2] Bishop Paul

Moore isolates three models for church cooperation. The first is the "organic unity" model. The East Harlem Protestant Parish is an excellent example of this type. The three men who undertook that project (two whites, one black) oriented the work toward social action. The evident needs of the community demanded not only aggressive action but an ecumenical witness. Anything short of this would have proven inadequate and irrelevant. In response to the task and because this was a completely new venture, it was rather easy to effect organic unity and transcend the usual barriers.

A second model would be that of "federation" in which churches decide to join with each other in sharing facilities, personnel, and finances. They do not begin *de novo* like the East Harlem Parish but bring with them to the "marriage" a long history and sometimes varied heritage. These may, in fact, be old established churches which have seen better days. They may stop short of complete organic unity as each former congregation may wish to maintain ties with its parent judicatory. The intent of federation is ecumenism.

The third model cited is that of "organized cooperation." It is this idea that I am primarily promoting. There is no attempt at organic union but rather cooperation on an organized basis in some area of the program of each supporting church, such as in social work or in education. Other areas, such as the worship experience, may maintain their separate identity. Of course, such cooperation may lead to federation and ecumenism. But in this model, it begins as limited, but planned cooperation.

When churches truly become conversant with and involved in the problems present in their community, there is often created a new awareness of the need for concerted action by the several churches located in the area. As long as a congregation refuses to address itself to the conditions under which its constituency is forced to live or refuses to see the plight of the poor, those enslaved by drugs, or those victimized by oppression, it is a fairly easy matter for them to assume that they are doing well alone and on their own. The enormity and complexity of the social problems of our time are beyond the abilities of individual parishes to deal with them effectively.

Not only the gospel, but the times in which we exist demand church cooperation. If we are serious when we say that the world sets the agenda for the church (at least in part—the gospel also determines our agenda) then we shall seek to answer the anguished cry of the world in the strongest manner that is possible.

Community organizations and civic clubs have long recognized the power that comes through joint strategy and effort. When the forces of evil seem well entrenched and organized, it becomes imperative that the forces for good also be together in purpose and in their actions. One way in which the churches could help themselves and their community is suggested in Stephen Rose's book *The Grass Roots Church*.[3] Where there is a cluster of churches in a community, one church might serve as the center for education, another for counseling services, and still another could be the center for recreation and community activities. Especially in urban areas, it is all but tragic that four churches on four corners would all be serving a few people and duplicating one another's efforts. This kind of "waste" can be ill-afforded by the church or by the community. In such situations, cooperation and coordination simply make for sensible service to the people involved. Here the church can exercise real leadership and serve as a model for the neighborhood.

In conclusion, I would restate the case. The legitimate reasons for cooperative ventures are not the popular ones that usually motivate us. Joint celebrations of festival and "high religious days" must be carefully analyzed, for these occasions may result from less than worthy motives. Moreover, they may serve to truncate the more vital and legitimate needs of church cooperation by serving as substitutes for more meaningful engagement. Rather, shared celebration may grow out of shared experiences of community involvement.

After an examination of God's mission in the world, and of the task of the Christian church in light of that mission, churches will work together as a response to the demands of the gospel. For if we are to be faithful to what God is doing in the world, e.g., reconciling men to one another, then the church dare not be an obstacle in his way! A second motivation for cooperation that seems justified is the church's response to the demands of the world. As we perceive the complexity and the interweaving of the issues we face, and our impotence to act individually and unilaterally, we cooperate in order to address ourselves to the needed changes in our society in a more effective manner.

Thus, from positions of relative strength and not through coercion, it is good to see denominations agreeing to cooperate and work together because they feel the gospel demands it and because the times beg for it. This is the approach of the co-operative evangelistic thrust called Key 73 and it is a worthy goal. The day has come when we must thoroughly understand that churches promoting ecumenism and/or working together toward a common goal is not just an optional strategy which we may or may not adopt. I strongly urge that this must become our priority. To ignore this task is to do so at our peril, for we shall be ignoring the biblical hope, that there shall be one fold and one shepherd.

---

1. Paul L. Stagg, *The Converted Church* (The Judson Press, 1967).
2. Paul Moore, Jr., *The Church Reclaims the City* (The Seabury Press, Incorporated, 1964).
3. Stephen C. Rose, *The Grass Roots Church* (Holt, Rinehart and Winston, 1966).

Questions for Reflection

1. What is God trying to do in the world?
2. What is the mission of the church in the world?
3. How can my local church relate to other local churches in common mission and ministry?

5

A Panel Responds

I

I am Raoul Calkins. I would like to make a comment on this matter of how cooperative endeavors can continue. I would agree with you 100 percent that unless we involve laymen in it, it collapses pretty rapidly and that if we involve laymen it seems to me that it goes faster and to greater depths. I have experienced it in both ways and I'm sure that if we are going to have grass roots cooperation in meeting various problems that we have got to involve laymen. I can illustrate this from two different ventures. I was pastor of a church in a white suburban community of 60,000 people. Not a single black family lived in this community. This was Kettering, the power structure suburb of Dayton.

There was a disturbance when a black family moved into the west side of Dayton in a semisuburban community and we didn't want to have that happen in "good ole Kettering." So we got together, ministers and priests, and discussed the matter as to a statement that we might make. I think we were afraid that if we got the laymen in we couldn't get it made! So we prepared a statement and purchased an advertisement page in the newspapers of the Dayton Area saying that it wasn't a matter of whether minority groups were going to move into the South Dayton Area or not, but whether we were going to treat them as Christians when they came. Now this was about what it amounted to and that was about it.

Some of us got to thinking about this later and in the church I was in we decided that we would try to gather together 100 persons both black and white. We had to import the blacks from other parts of Dayton! We divided them up into ten different groups. About 80 showed up—with 8 or 10 in each group. Now, this consisted almost exclusively of lay people, and no one could become a part of this unless he agreed to give the time to meet for six consecutive weeks, at least once a week in terms of working together and getting acquainted. These lay persons wanted to see some action!

You know we ministers, many times, are willing to talk and make a pronouncement but they wanted action. And this was interdenominational. It wasn't started as such, but we did get into each one of these groups various Christian persons—a Roman Catholic, a Presbyterian, United Methodist, etc. This group with their concern for action formed an organization that was ecumenical in nature. Only one minister was related to it—the rest were laymen and out of this there came not only an open occupancy ordinance for the three areas south of Dayton but also the implementation for aiding persons to move into the community. A pronouncement by the ministers didn't do any harm but when the laymen got involved in it that was an entirely different ball game. And I think this is imperative.

Now also on this matter of ecumenical relationships on a grass roots level, it doesn't do any good to say, "This is what we want you to do, you come and join us!" I am serving now as the executive secretary for the quadrennial emphasis Fund for Reconciliation. The General Conference of 1968 said that we should endeavor to have as many ecumenical involvements as possible so that the Fund for Reconciliation ministry would be multiplied. I have been observing this pretty carefully. From the contact I have personally and through writing with some 780 projects The United Methodist Church is carrying on across the country at the present time, *the only ones of these that are ecumenical in nature as far as I can discover are where—before the project was instituted a group of concerned persons was brought together and said, "What should we do?"* But if someone says, "This is what The United Methodist Church wants to do and wouldn't you Presbyterians, Episcopalians, etc. etc, like to cooperate with us in doing this project"—it just doesn't happen. We have to start at the grass roots in terms of saying, "This is the task that we have before us. Isn't this something that we really ought to tackle in our community? Now, how can we tackle it together?" And then the thing can really go. But for us to say, "Come and join us," that's the sure way to kill anything on the grass roots level of an ecumenical nature.

Raoul Calkins is Executive Secretary for the quadrennial emphasis Fund for Reconciliation of The United Methodist Church.

II

I am Gene Coffin. I feel a little bit like a fish out of water here as the only non-Methodist on the panel. You scare me, but as a Quaker I guess I'll have to settle for still being in the minority and express my appreciation for the opportunity of sharing with you today. I have been serving as an executive secretary in evangelism for our international work for the past 7 years, I've gone back to the local church now because I do not want to lose touch with the grass roots and I suppose that's one reason I am here. I'd like to make a comment on George Outen's reference to the fact that the civil league took some corporate action in that particular situation on which were a number of members of the church. I am sure you were inferring this but would like to underline it that the accomplishment of the civic league in getting rid of that taproom was really the church working together. It was an illustration of this cooperative thing. Just because the clergy is not involved doesn't mean the church was not involved. These Christian people were working together in a secular organization. I think we preachers have exploited our vested interests too much to the frustration of the grace of God in many places simply by identifying ourselves as the only ones who are the institutional representatives. I am sure this is what you are implying.

I would like to say that there are a lot of weeds grown up in the grass roots that we have to get rid of if we are actually going to have cooperative evangelism. People do not want to get together and work together as churches in many places. Take the rural situation. Try to get some rural churches together. I am sure you in Methodism have a lot of small churches in the country which maintain their identity and refuse to merge or even cooperate with other Methodists in the area.

We have this in the Friends Church, I'll have to confess, and so we need an ecumenical Quakerism as well as an ecumenical Christianity! You probably need an ecumenical Methodism, I don't know. But the point is, are we willing really to get at this practical problem of people not really wanting to work together simply because they have been identified with their little group and don't want to be identified in any larger way. We need to root out some weeds. I appreciate the emphasis that the church is people and the church building is just a place where the church meets. Bruce Larson has reminded us that we need to build a relational theology, which sounds like a forward-looking task. Through action together we can build that relational theology and root out the weeds of provincialism.

Let me comment on the Youth Revolt in the world and in the country and in the church which I believe is one of the most hopeful signs for our time! That is, young people are saying, "We are tired of these old battles that you older folks have been fighting. Let's get on with the work of the Lord." Here is a clue to some ecumenical relationships which I think we can develop through our youth movements. They are saying "right on" and I think we ought to get right on with it.

The areas where we can perhaps work together have to do with the issues that our young people are facing. We are finding in the Friends Church, and I expect you are in The United Methodist Church, a very real need to interpret the conscientious objection position. We could do a real job of service together in an interpretation of the rights of young people at this point. We could work together, too, in a ministry to the military which denominations are doing and the chaplain's corps is doing.

We can work together for the elimination of the drug problem. We have a situation in La Habra, California, where the youth center of that particular city became the focal point for vandalism and drug distribution. The city had to close it down. A number of us got together and developed a concern for what is now called *The Vine. The Vine*, which is again a youth center, is definitely based upon a Christian premise that the miracle of God's Grace can release and set a person free from the use of drugs. In getting together on this kind of premise, the city allowed the use of the recreation center on a temporary basis to see how it works. This is happening in spite of opposition from the community. At a Thursday morning breakfast across denominational lines, laymen (only one or two pastors are involved) have been working together to support this idea.

We have enlisted a doctor, a psychiatrist, a psychologist and legal counsel to be on the team. Their involvement helps establish credibility in the community as they are able to confirm the miracle of God's Grace in the release of young people from the drug habit. This is cooperative evangelism as far as I am concerned. These kids are turned on! They had a birthday party for Jesus the other day, and there were about 500 people who came to see what God was doing. When we get this kind of excitement, this kind of support, this kind of credibility documented for the community then I think we are beginning to get at some of the real issues.

Two spiritual principles I want to mention. One is "Except a corn of wheat fall on the ground and die it abideth alone, but if it die it bringeth forth fruit." Unless this principle is planted in the heart of every Christian, the weeds of denominational competition will not be rooted out. We are competing with one another in many ways, let's face it. Jesus said, "I will make you fishers of men." Instead of trading members and calling it evangelism, we ought to get out and reach the unreached where they are. The second principle is "Agape"; love which is given without expectation of return. We have become so commercial about our evangelism that statistics (the return) overshadow and even blot out the love which motivates evangelism. In this way we have adopted the world's way to do the Kingdom's work. We need to root out the weeds of self-interest. The issues are so great you see, that the dynamics of the demonic forces which are at work in our churches as well as in the world are so penetrating that nothing short of obedience to the Holy Spirit will equip us for cooperative evangelism.

Eugene Coffin served for several years as Executive Secretary for Evangelism in the Friends Church. He is now minister of East Whittier Friends Church in Whittier, California.

III

I am Peter Misner. I'd like to comment on the reference that our coming together in cooperative evangelism is more desirable out of strength than out of weakness. I think that's very much to be desired, but I'm sure that a great part of our experience is that we honestly come together out of weakness rather than out of strength, simply because when we are feeling strong, when we are really on top of it, we do not feel the need for others. This is the kind of arrogance and closedness that has stifled holding out our hand to anyone else, either to give or to receive. I think you were saying that in your summing up. But I wanted to make special reference to it because that's been a part of my experience.

The other comment that I would want to make is that somehow in our ecumenical strategy we've been reading a number of statements about the identity crisis among persons as individuals, and certainly we are facing an identity crisis in our institutional life as well. It seems to me that one of our motivations for ecumenical evangelism is to share the gifts that are a part of each of our traditions in such a loving way, that we can help each other to discover who we are. I heard a speaker say not long ago that he never really knew what it was to be a man until he had a wife. And he said, "My wife continually tells me what it is to be a male, what it is to be a husband, what it is to be a person." It seems to me that a part of the great gift that we have to share as United Methodists is who we are in the whole spectrum of the Christian church, and receiving the same kind of insights from others which will help us to know more clearly who we are. If we are to laud The United Methodist Church as an end in itself, as we tended to do in the past, then we are just going about our arrogant way in isolation. But I think we are at a point where we can begin to say out of our weakness, out of our awareness, that we really don't know who we are unless somebody else tells us. Then we can begin to be truly the church of Jesus Christ. I pray for that. That is the direction in which we have been working.

Peter Misner is Director of Ecumenical Evangelism involving Protestant, Catholic, and Orthodox churches in the New England area.

IV

I am Gerald Trigg. I have been a little disappointed not in what has happened here, but what has not happened in this group when we come to talk about ecumenical ventures and we sit here as United Methodists alone and we never get outside that category. Where is the mention of COCU at a time that is supposed to be the study period for the plan of union at the local level? Here is an opportunity for grass roots study across denominational lines that will enable us to penetrate some of the myths that we have entertained about the local church and its essence, superiority and talk about the strengths and weaknesses at the local level. It would have helped me enormously, I think, to have had some keen suggestions forthcoming during this session as to how we could best have made that work at the local level.

Something of encouragement and discouragement has come through the fact that at least we have gathered to talk about the evangelistic mission in our day. I am grateful, Dr. Outen, for your presentation of "what is the mission" and especially for striking the note of "Kingdom" consciousness. We have had so many people hung up on the local church, assuming that was the last word from God, when in reality the church, as I view it, is simply and solely an instrument of the Kingdom, nothing more nor less, and not the only instrument, but one that may or may not be helpful from time to time. The mission must be to the world.

I have appreciated enormously Bruce Larson's comments that have led us into a new awareness of the freedom that is ours in the faith, and I have been frankly more uplifted, my soul stirred more, by the possibilities of what the church might be, through this man's presentation, than through any other note that's been struck. I like to hear this word that suggests that maybe the mission of the church has moved from the pre-emphasis or primary emphasis on *conversion* to an emphasis on *concern*, for it may well be that the church's real mission is *not* conversion. In fact I would like for somebody to show me in the Scripture somewhere where that is the church's mission. I think the church's mission is to witness and to nurture, but let God bring the conversion through his

Holy Spirit; which means that on the continuum of conversion there must come the witness, then the conversion by the Holy Spirit, and then the nurture. Now the church has been all hung up in its evangelism on trying to get converts, but it has not been willing to witness, it has not been willing to nurture and to lead people into an awareness of what it's all about once they have been led to some kind of decision.

I'm delighted to hear the note struck too that we need not be so interested in success, "trying to tally up the figures," but rather trust, be faithful, do what you have to do, then leave the consequences in the hands of God.

If we could have also heard, and I think we have been hearing it though not as clearly as I would have liked, some note that suggests that we ought to move from our emphasis on social welfare, as we have had that in the church, to social justice in which we cooperatively manifest this. Now I'd love to see this take place on the grass roots level. I have been involved in this my last three pastorates: one in a changing neighborhood, one in an inner city; and I gave the suburban churches hell so much that the bishop moved me to a suburban church and I'm there now!

We've been able to get some things going ecumenically. We now, for example, have incorporated in our community a Center for Lay Ministries that is tackling a number of things, including a coffee-house for the hippie group in our community. That has been so successful that it's been closed down, because we were averaging 200-250 of these kids, many of them on drugs, each weekend and so the community has closed it. Now we've got to open it somewhere else. We had that going in a shopping center, incidentally.

We've had a family film festival that moved over the community, weekly Disney films, shown for families where they have had difficulty getting good viewing. We have the Contact (Life-line) telephone ministry now in the preparatory stages. We've got Fish, which is the "Be a Neighbor Program," counseling underway, a Dialogue with the World Film Series, a series of things that have been taking place ecumenically. It has been very encouraging to me to see laymen giving leadership across denominational lines, and we are really looking forward to the COCU studies this year which are going to be held throughout our community, across racial lines, across denominational lines and in small groups. If we mix enough of our congregations we've got commitments from three of the pastors of the largest churches, that in a year or two we want to be one church in the community. This is a United Presbyterian, United Methodist and the Christian Church, Disciples of Christ. Now, whether it comes off remains to be seen but we are rather excited about it. I don't want to sound like an "ecumaniac" or a COCU-nut, but I think that it is important to say these days as Colin Morris wrote in his book, *Include Me Out*, "We can be interested in doing it ecumenically, we can do it individually, but for God's sake, do it."

Gerald Trigg is pastor of Morton Memorial United Methodist Church in Clarksville, Indiana.

V

I am W. T. Handy, Jr., a native of Louisiana. Being an avid sports fan I have been steeped in the LSU winning football tradition. The team is riding kind of high right now, but it has not always been like this. I can vividly remember when their fortunes were at a low ebb, to put it mildly. It got so bad back in the fifties that they finally fired the coach. Then they hired a young hot shot who was supposed to bring them out of the doldrums, set them on high and give them national prominence.

The coach's name was Paul Dietsel and he worked hard. The first year the team still did not fare too well. The next year it did even worse, won two and lost eight. The wolves began to howl. Finally at a press conference the sports writers raised some embarrassing questions. What had happened? Why was the record so bad after all the beginning promise? Had his program failed? After listening patiently for a while the young coach then responded, "If you want to make chicken salad, the first thing you've got to have is some chicken."

For some time I have been hearing talk about ecumenism, Christian cooperation in the Christian spirit for Christian ventures. We talk about the church needing to go out to do this and to do that as if we could just press a button and here goes the church marching like a mighty army. But, as I see it, we are dealing with people in the local churches who do not have this idea, this concept or whatever you want to call it that some of us seem to have. If we are going to talk about a chicken salad of mission, a chicken salad of Christian service, the first thing we must have is some chicken! And the chicken of the church is people, the people in the local church.

Who are these people in the church pews on Sunday, who are on the church rolls and whom some of us constantly berate as being spiritually shortsighted? These are the folk who don't have these ideas about the mission of the church as do some of us. They believe, and some of us have to a large extent led them to believe, that if you go up the aisle, give the preacher your hand, share in the singing, be sure to put money in the plate on Sunday morning, pay the church financial claims, etc., that's it. But is that it? I think we would agree that it is not. But have we taught these people, have we trained these people, have we loved these people enough? We've got to love them too! I wonder sometimes do we love them as much as we claim to love others and other causes. Sometimes it appears we love everybody else but them. But we need to love them too—they're also God's children. So often we use ecclesiastical jargon which they don't understand. At times we speak contemptuously and arrogantly to them.

I think that we should be thinking in terms of Christian service ecumenically. But sometimes I have problems with much of our ecumenism because I think much of our concern is about structure rather than service. This might be caused primarily because of survival. Are we thinking of people when we talk about new ventures, or are we concerned with projects or with new programs? Are we thinking about people and meeting their needs through service? Are we interested in being a minister or in rendering ministerial service? These are the things that concern me.

But to get back to my original statement. The first thing we need to do is to get some ecclesiastical chicken! In some circles the term "conversion" is passé. But when Nicodemus came by night to see Jesus, the master told him that something had to happen to him. It is my thinking that if this program is to become meaningful something will have to happen to the people.

Certainly I would not want to convey the impression that I condone personal conversion as the panacea for all the world's social ills. I would not want to be that much misunderstood. Surely I do not wish to project the idea that all we've got to do is get everybody converted and then render service. I'm not meaning that. But I am convinced that our basic problem is that we are endeavoring to make chicken ecumenism without the chicken. We've got to work with the people and try to help them understand what is the true mission of the church. I think that we can talk about denominational cooperation, ecumenism as much as we want, but without the people in the local church it is just going to be another program which will be promoted by the ecclesiastical hierarchy, the board executives, the big legislative and organizational bodies and then in time be dropped in favor of another program which will not reach the people.

Unless we change the procedures and practices of the past few years we will leave the conferences, the conventions, and the congresses, filled with high hopes and enthusiasm. The overriding question in my mind for ecumenism and cooperation at this time is, "We need the people for our hopes to come to fruition. How do we convey this enthusiasm and excitement to them?"

W. T. Handy, Jr. is vice-president in charge of personnel and public relations for the Methodist Publishing House in Nashville, Tennessee.

6

Literature, the Arts, and Evangelism

By David J. Williams

I want to begin by asking each of you to consider four questions which I think are preliminary to any discussion of cooperative evangelism, and in particular, those discussions related to the use of literature and the arts. (Let it be understood that I refer to both of these in the broadest sense. We are not necessarily talking about Scripture or other evangelistic materials. Nor are we talking about paintings and drawings per se. Rather when we talk about the arts we are talking about the performing arts, graphic arts, painting, photographic arts and all other forms of the arts which might come to mind.) The questions are: (1) What is my attitude toward the use of tracts and Scripture brochures as tools for evangelism in my ministry? (2) Do I view "secular" drama and art as a means of conveying a Christian message? (3) Do I ever consider the use of drama, dance, or the graphic and visual arts during a service of worship on Sunday morning, as a means of proclamation? And finally, (4) What is my attitude toward the proclamation of God's word in such public places as shopping centers, street corners, and city or town parts?

The reason I am asking you to consider these questions is because, as I pondered the whole question of the use of literature and the arts in a program of cooperative evangelism, it seemed to me that these questions reflect basic hang-ups which we often have about certain methods of proclamation employed by churches other than our own. If you review the four questions you probably will be able to think of some groups that use one type of these methods over against the others and who feel more comfortable with them than we do. By raising the question, I wanted each of you to have the opportunity to think through your own posture and convictions about these methods.

If we are going to engage in cooperative evangelism utilizing literature and the arts on any scale, then we have to be prepared to confront, realistically, our anxieties about certain ways of doing evangelism. We must overcome certain prejudices which too often, by their very nature, direct our work of witness *inward* rather than *outward*. Often what we call evangelism is really revivalism, concentrating on the renewal of the already committed rather than the winning of the uncommitted. Time and time again, our discussions in the local church focus around what we are doing for ourselves and how we can stimulate the local church life. This kind of discussion is born out of the traditional concept of "Live and let live." The "Live and let live" concept makes many of us feel uncomfortable about going out onto street corners or to shopping centers and making a witness. We do not want to impose our view upon another, even though we believe that Jesus Christ is the redeemer of all mankind. This concept of ignoring the neighbor while saving the self has no place in a church which is concerned for the whole fabric of mankind.

We live in a world the very nature of which brings to the fore the basest elements of the human mentality. The problems of coping with modern technology and the pace of contemporary life, place each of us under stress and strain which is too often more than we are capable of standing. As I flew to New Orleans yesterday, I had a five-hour delay because of weather conditions. My emotions spilled over in exasperation and I lost the ability to deal sensibly with the problem. Finally when we got under way, I opened my paper and tried to unwind but I was confronted with various elements of the news which continued to undermine my calm. On one page was a review of a play which had opened the evening before. The title "Stag Film" gives you an idea about the nature of the play and from the reviews, one gathered that the play was quite explicit. I read the reviews and was interested to discover that one reviewer condemned it out-of-hand, as bad drama, but said nothing about the morality of the play. Another paper's reviewer said it had some redeeming qualities about it but that it would not survive very long, and a third reviewer took a similar attitude. No one was particularly concerned about the morality of the actions that took place on the stage.

Over against this creeping erosion of traditional values, we have the message of the church and a Christian perspective which we claim and which we share with one another. However, we must see that while our perspective is set against the perspective of the world, it is not to run from it. We must associate with the perspective of the world because we are concerned and our concern is born out of our compassion for a world which is steadily deteriorating. We cannot run from the world saying, "tut, tut" and hide in our closets. Rather we must look at the world with a yearning to make it new and fresh. In fact, we might use a phrase from a brochure a friend sent me: "In the same old bag, fresh cookies." Christians are called to put fresh cookies in the world and to do so, we are called to move forward into new realms of evangelism and new methods of witnessing.

If our ministry of evangelism is a ministry of compassion then it is a ministry to a world of persons whose needs and concerns are our needs and concerns, persons with whom we can identify. Our concern turns our witness outward in evangelism rather than inward in revival. We must say to the world in the most contemporary fashion possible, "I want to share with you something that has had a great deal of meaning for my life." I believe that that phrase is the key thought to bear in mind when doing evangelism and being concerned with the spreading of the message of Jesus Christ. Unless we preface everything that we are doing with that concept, then I do not think we are engaged in evangelism.

I first heard those words, incidentally, from Bill Wade, the football player, in a night club in Florida as part of an Easter ministry in Daytona Beach. He was a member of a team that was making a witness and after he had shared with the audience of college students the reason why he had come to

Daytona Beach for Easter week and what Jesus Christ meant to him, he held up a copy of the "Sermon on the Mount" and said, "Now, I want to share with you something that has had a great deal of meaning for my life. We are not just going to pass them out to everyone, but if you would like a copy of the 'Sermon on the Mount' from the New Testament, raise your hand and we will hand you a copy." We went to three night clubs and gave away 250 copies of the "Sermon on the Mount." The success of that evening as well as the success of all that we do in evangelism is predicated on the investment of the Christian individual in the message of Jesus Christ. Bill Wade endorsed Christianity with his witness! He invested himself by taking his message where the action was and by sharing it with others. He reached out and touched the world rather than running from it.

The Christian is called to a schizophrenic existence which requires us to speak to sister Sue in the pew as well as the man on the street. Clergy and laity alike experience this schizophrenic existence in the local church—the schizophrenia of trying to minister to people who understand the language of the church and find it meaningful and to minister to persons who do not hear because they are not attuned to our special language even though some of them may have a religious background. I would like to suggest that literature and the arts may be two of the communicating bridges across which the message of Jesus Christ can be sent to the man in the pew and the man in the street.

Where do we begin to incorporate into the ministry of the church, these two possible communication methods? Most of us have the tools at hand and we do not recognize them. Let me give you a case in point. This fall, I was invited to speak to the Women's Society of Christian Service of a large United Methodist Church in the New York Conference. They had asked me to come and speak to them on the theme, "How the Word Gets Around." As I entered the lounge in which they held their meetings my eye was immediately drawn to two large banners hanging in the room. They were typical of the large banners being made by so many church groups. These particular banners had beeen made by two of the Circles, and they were quite proud of them. As I began to speak, I said, "I like this banner and in particular I like its message that 'The Church has been quiet too long,' but why is it hanging here?" The women looked rather perplexed but one of them finally said, "Well it's hanging there so everyone can see it." And, I said, "Whom do you mean by everyone?" "Well, everybody in the church," she replied. I smiled and suggested that the next day a few of them go down the road about a quarter of a mile to the shopping center and speak to some of the store managers to see if they would display the banner so that indeed everybody could see it. Here was an effort at proclamation, an effort to say something, but its scope was limited by the place the women had chosen to hang their proclamation. They had a limited vision about where they could make their proclamation and this is the problem throughout the church. The fault is not theirs but ours as those who are concerned for the life of the church.

Begin where you are! Look about you for the opportunities which are in the very midst of your local church life. Expand your vision so that it looks beyond the four walls of the church into the community. If you have banners to display there is a good chance that other churches in your area have some of their own. Here is an opportunity for cooperative evangelism at the grass roots level. Contact the churches, organize an exhibit of the banners in a prominent public location such as a bank lobby or a movie lobby, or a department store window.

What about community-wide arts festivals? Dozens of communities across the country will probably have such festivals this year and the number will grow in the years to come. The churches can cooperate with the local arts committee by sponsoring a Christian art exhibit during the festival; not down in some dark church basement or shoved off in the corner of the education building, but out in a public location where people can see the art and reflect on it. We need to get these things out of the churches and into the streets, into the *agora*, the market place, and the banks.

We have a wonderful resource in the churches—the people who have responsible business positions as bank managers, movie owners, auto dealers, and department store owners. One of those resources can be approached: "Say, John Doe, we are having a community arts festival and the Council of Churches is cooperating by sponsoring an exhibit of Christian art. You know that if we have it in the basement of the church no one is going to come except our own people. Could we have some space in the bank lobby for two weeks?" If he asks why you want it out of the church, tell him you want to confront nonchurched people so that they will start thinking about Christian truths.

In hanging the exhibit it would be well to accompany each painting with a statement. This statement should describe the artist's feelings as he developed his painting so that the viewer has some idea what was happening in the mind of the painter. For example, one day I walked into the apartment of Elizabeth Korn, a retired professor of art from Drew University where I did my undergraduate work. We have been friends for a number of years and I know her mind and its workings quite well. Therefore when I saw a new painting all in blues and golds, I knew it could only be a Madonna. When I asked her about the painting, she said that she had come home quite depressed one day and began to think of her childhood. She thought of the churches in Eastern Europe which were so quiet and serene and she thought of the big statues of the Madonna. In her moment of depression the comfort of those early moments had come back to her and she had to paint the moment. Such information accompanying a painting in an exhibit could be a powerful witness to someone who thinks the serenity of the life in Jesus Christ is a myth.

We have all had the experience of coming home from a church function and discovering a friend or neighbor who would have gone had he known about it. This failure of communication was brought home to me following an Easter sunrise service when a friend said he would have gone if he had only known there was a service. I began to think about the problem of getting the message out when I was in the local church, but it is only recently that I began to see one possible solution to the problem. In many communities the churches sponsor the Easter service as a joint effort, and through this joint sponsorship a certain amount of goodwill has been established in the community. In these communities it may be possible to go to the local high school teacher of art, or adult education teacher of art and say, "We do not want you to do this in your classroom but we would like to have you announce to your students that the churches of this community are sponsoring a design competition on the theme of Easter. We would like to have entries from as many people as possible— both youth and adults—and from these we are going to choose a design for use on posters throughout the town and also we will use it on the cover of a bulletin for the Easter service." Think for a moment about the possible results of such a move. I can see dozens of people who may not have been near the Scriptures in years, sitting down to read the Easter story in preparation for their design. I can see these same people trying to work through the ideas suggested by the text.

I can see a pastor or layman announcing a discussion group on the meaning of Easter for all those artists who want to come and discuss the meaning of Easter and the relevancy of the Easter story to contemporary life.

I see a Christian art teacher taking this opportunity to express her Christian faith on a one-to-one basis with some of her students in the public schools. A student comes along and indicates that he would like to get involved but does not know how to get started. Here is an opportunity for a Christian layman or laywoman who cannot say anything about Jesus Christ in her classroom to become an evangelist to this young person. The avenues which might open up for a witness during such a community project are too numerous to mention. What is required is imagination and vision to seize the available opportunities.

We have talked about the graphic arts but there are certainly many opportunities for evangelistic use of the performing arts. Many communities have active drama groups within the local churches. What would happen if these groups turned their energies occasionally from the lighthearted comedies and talent shows which seem to be filling their schedules to the production of several one act Christian dramas suitable for performance on a flat bed truck in a shopping center? I am not suggesting a biblical play in "bathrobe" costuming but rather works by such authors as Charles Williams and Christopher Fry. The performance of such meaningful works in a public place on a busy Saturday morning would be a worthy enterprise and would use the talent already available in so many churches.

I have mentioned that there is another bridge which could be used to communicate to both the pew and the man in the street, and that is literature.

Recently I was manning an exhibit booth and as people passed the table my colleague and I offered them a copy of a Scripture selection entitled "Good News for Louisiana" and containing part of the "Sermon on the Mount." Somebody passing by said, "Is this a tract?" I replied, "No, it's Scripture." He said, "I'll take it." His attitude demonstrates very well the kind of suspicion and hangups which we have about certain methods of evangelism. I am convinced that the hangup stems from the way that people do the distribution rather than from the material used. I see small selections of Scripture in attractive colorful formats as being a tool for grass roots evangelism. But we are not going to be able to make effective use of Scripture or other material in "tract" format unless we can rid ourselves of our prejudices regarding this method of evangelism.

Last year 99 million copies of the Scripture were distributed by the American Bible Society through the churches and individuals of this country. Some of this Scripture was probably not too effectively distributed and found its way into the waste basket, but the letters in the files of the American Bible Society testify to the effective use of a great deal of Scripture being made by creative persons. The stories which come in the mail every day testify to the fact that God is using the Scripture as a powerful evangelistic tool. Hippie communes write and request copies of *Good News for Modern Man* to share with others; young people pass up and down the route of the Rose Parade the night before distributing Scripture and talking with those who are waiting for the parade; a drug addict is confronted with the message of Jesus Christ and gets turned on to a new kind of life; in the locker of a football player killed in a tragic airplane crash is found a copy of a New Testament filled with notes and underlinings—his roommate spoke about the boy at his funeral and told how they used to read to each other from the New Testament each evening; a performer in an annual Passion Play in the midwest distributed New Testaments to members of the cast, and to customers in his barber shop; a car dealer places a Scripture in each glove compartment; a banker provides a copy of the Psalms for each customer with whom he deals; and a realtor gives each person buying a home a New Testament.

The success of the distribution cited above goes back to Bill Wade's statement. No one will read what we give him unless he thinks that it has some meaning for the person asking him to read it.

In San Antonio, during a ministry at the Hemisfair, I said to the youth participants who were distributing Scripture that I did not want a single piece of Scripture distributed on the fair ground that was not accompanied by some word about how much that Scripture meant to them. I pointed out to them that we had to recommend the word with the same eagerness that we recommend a particular brand of car or household detergent. We are so willing to endorse all manner of products that we use to make our life physically comfortable, but rarely do we recommend that which brings comfort to our spiritual life.

Large Scripture distribution projects have been carried out on a cooperative basis by the Council of Churches in several areas. In November, 1970, 750,000 copies of *Good News for Modern Man* were distributed door-to-door by the churches of South Carolina under the direction of the Christian Action Council of that state. The churches acting together raised the money that was required for this project because they were convinced that the distribution of God's word was one project in which all churches could cooperate. A project in Illinois called for the distribution of half a million Testaments in April 1971. In other communities around the country, laymen are engaging in evangelism by going out and calling on their neighbors and friends to tell them what God has done for them and how they want to share God's word with them.

Recently, a layman in Columbia, South Carolina, called the

American Bible Society and told one of the executives that the Bible Society had just published one of the best greeting cards ever. He was referring to a ten cent edition of the Psalms for the bereaved, the sick, and the rejoicing.

A number of companies, including denominational presses, are producing attractive and meaningful tracts for distribution and the same guidelines suggested for distribution of the Scriptures apply to these tracts. If we are going to give somebody something, then we should share ourselves with it.

There is another guideline which I would suggest. Some are so eager to share their faith that they overwhelm people not only with their testimony but with literature. Make it a practice to judge where people are so that you do not overwhelm them. At the Bible Society, we suggest that it is better to give a Gospel to a new Christian rather than a whole Testament or Bible. They need to find their way and be comfortable. If you give a whole Bible to a person who does not know how to find his way in it, he will give up in frustration. The same is true in making testimony. Every theological doctrine need not be explained the first time around. Each person must have the opportunity to grow in his faith. In a way the people of the world who live where translation work on the Bible is still going on, may be better off than those of us who live in an affluent society, because they come to love and appreciate the Scriptures in manageable segments. They can bite off smaller bits and digest them.

The same thing holds true for selecting other literature for evangelism and discussion. Begin where you find a person and do not overwhelm him.

So far I have talked only about the use of religious literature. There is, however, a potential for witness in much of the secular literature of our times. Many communities have literary groups and book clubs which meet on a regular basis. The discussion at these meetings often does not go any deeper than the story line of the book. It would seem to me that an alert, knowledgeable Christian could use the discusssion to witness to the Christian perspective of life and how it relates to the material being discussed. We need to be concerned when we read contemporary literature to bring to it in a conscious fashion our faith. In sharing our reflections we may lead someone to an understanding of the importance of Christ for his life. Such reflection is particularly important when dealing with books which are totally negative in their approach to life. When reading such a book as *The Love Machine* one must begin with the question, "What does this book say about man?" From this the possibilities for discussion and witness are endless.

All the foregoing material is certainly not meant to cover the entire realm of possibilities for the use of the arts and literature in evangelism. It is meant to be suggestive of ways in which we can use these tools in personal as well as cooperative evangelism. The method that we use will be dictated by the unique situation in which the church finds itself. The determination of what method is appropriate may be the most difficult task of all. Confronted with a rapidly changing world which must be ministered to, and at the same time attempting to preserve the world of those who now are within the fellowship of the church, it will be the laymen who will determine how well the local churches adapt. The church's ministry is determined by the attitudes of the laymen and there will be no fresh cookies in the same old world unless the witness of the laymen puts them there.

I live in a neighborhood which contains some of the most diverse and deviate elements of an urban society. Drug addiction, prostitution, homosexuality, theft, and robbery are common. The traditional methods of communicating the gospel are not reaching and will not reach the persons in our society who are involved in these activities. New ways and fresh methods may possibly make a difference. It is not uncommon for my phone to ring at 3:00 A.M. and for me to be confronted with the voice of one who is terrified to death because of the effects a certain drug is having on him, or because of what some other condition of life is doing to him. He does not look for an easier answer but rather for a willingness to listen and to hear what he is saying. A church which is seeking to serve the message of Jesus Christ in the world must have that same openness to listen if it is going to find how to communicate his good news to the world.

The confusion of the neighborhood in which I live is the confusion of the world in microcosm. The identical problems do not exist everywhere but the essential confusion exists. The way of dealing with the confusion is to listen and ask the appropriate questions of ourselves: questions which will yield meaningful answers. Until we ask these questions we will continue to be frustrated in our search for ways of ministering to the world.

The problem of the church in suburbia is not the problem of the urban church and the problem of the urban church is not the problem of the rural church. In the larger denominations the emphasis has been too often on a national church creating a national program for the church as a whole. This approach will not do for the twenty-first century because it stifles creative thinking within the local situation. It is this creative thinking within the local situation that will be the most difficult of tasks and which will produce the most rewarding results. New forms of ministry will be accepted when they are born out of the labor of the local church searching together to meet the needs of the community. The blood pressure of some goes up when they see a magazine article about dancing in the church chancel or about a ministry to a subculture of our society and yet those ministries are born out of a search on a local level for ways to minister to the needs of people where they are physically and spiritually. If the church is to survive into the next century the search for new ministries must begin in every community. I have tried to suggest some new ministries, but I add this word of caution. In the search for the way forward, let us not forget that the method is the tool by which we make Christ known and not an end in itself. Too often we have come to revere the method of our working more than him for whom we work.

Questions for Reflection

1. How is my church using art forms for Christian proclamation? How can wider use be made?
2. What strategies might be employed to encourage wider distribution of the Scriptures in my community?

7

Proclamation Via Mass Media?

By Ronn Kerr

Can proclamation take place via the mass media? On the surface, this seems a simple question with an equally simple answer. "Yes," we say, "the existence of mass media is one of the most significant facts in the modern world and it is an obvious vehicle for communicating God's word to the rapidly growing masses."

Daily, we encounter persons who point to mass media—especially its broadcast varieties—as the ultimate solution to the problem of mass evangelism. There is a "toy department" philosophy present in much of the church that believes unquestionably that some ultimate potential for the arrival of the Kingdom came with the icon advent. Not unlike the salesmanship, public relations, motivational analysis, and sensitivity training fetishes that periodically rear their heads in evangelism circles, the "we-can-save-them-through-television" mindset grows, I suspect, out of a basic fear of one-to-one confrontation and witness.

The idea of proclamation via the mass media is fraught with complications. In addition to the massive difficulties in communicating the gospel from man to man, mass media adds a complicating medium in between the two communicating parties. Potentially two-way communication is restricted to one-way. The one-to-one concept suddenly becomes one to millions. And, the usual interference present in any communications system is multiplied by machinery, by space and time, and by the involvement of a wider variety of people.

86

In the following, we will first look at the process of Christian witnessing and isolate some of the problems it presents for mass media proclamation. Then, we will look at some of the reasons why, even with problems, we must attempt to proclaim via mass media. And finally, we will look at some broad things that must be done in order to use media effectively for mass evangelism.

The great potential of mass media as a vehicle for teaching, for distributing information and for persuading has been adequately proven by commerce and government. And in these areas, it has been a successful vehicle for the church as well. But isn't proclamation of God's saving grace something more than even a combination of teaching, distributing information and persuading? I think so.

This can be illustrated, I believe, by relating the role of the Christian proclaimer to the role of the artist as a communicator. The difference between a craftsman and an artist is very similar to the difference between bread-'n'-butter communication of information and the proclamation of the Christian gospel.

The artist, God, and the witnessing Christian have at least five things in common. First, in each case, they choose to extend themselves and represent themselves in an act of love through a medium. The artist chooses one of the artistic media such as paint, stone, poetry, or film through which he shares a unique part of himself in a self-giving act. God saw that man needed a means by which he could more easily identify and understand the nature of the Father. God, therefore, extended and represented himself in a medium by incarnating himself in the man Jesus of Nazareth. Through this act, he provided some tangible awareness of the nature of God for you and me.

As witnesses we too are called to extend and represent ourselves as God's agents. Through speech and actions (our media) we extend ourselves in an act of love to share the best of all possible good news to a hungry people.

Whether or not the full impact of the Christian witness in both word and deed can be expressed indirectly and impersonally via mass media is questionable. Can we find ways in which persons come to feel God's love and acceptance which are removed from the authority of personal contact? Can persons come to accept that they are loved by God without making direct contact with the life and love of a witnessing Christian?

Second, the artist attempts both to communicate the truth and express inexpressible ideas. One kind of truth is "twelve inches makes a foot." This is a provable truth. But some kinds of truth can only be experienced. For instance, most persons can attest to the truth of love and hate and jealousy and joy but these are, for the empirical minded, inexpressible realities. They are, however, the everyday fuel for the artist's creative machinery. Art happens when an inexpressible idea is transmitted, frequently without definition, from artist to aesthete via an experiential event of some kind. God, too, is an inexpressible reality. In order to communicate himself to us, he chose to represent himself in Jesus the Christ through whom we experience the love of God.

The Christian witness has a similar challenge—to express the inexpressible. In the minds of modern pagans, the coded language of the Christian faith has come to be identified with a kind of folk religion of nationalism, clean living and gentlemanly behavior. With the language of the faith so impoverished and misunderstood, it is questionable whether or not the good news can be described or illustrated without some experiential involvement, especially when the transmission of the message is via mass media.

Third, the work of the artist can truly be called art only when the *form* in which his message is conveyed is in absolute harmony with the *content* of the message. Following this rule, the Incarnation is certainly "the artwork of Almighty God," as St. Augustine wrote. God chose to express his message of love and forgiveness in the person of Jesus Christ. The *content* of love came to us in the *form* of an all-loving man.

This formula also has merit for understanding Christian witness. What form can our witness take that will be in harmony with the content of the good news we have to offer? Obviously, only a life that embodies the love of God and neighbor has any basis of authority for witness and, therefore, the perfect form of the Christian message is an expression of unmerited love. Can love, as well as information, be transmitted via the mass media? Or, can the gospel be effective when transmitted in a less than perfect form?

Fourth, the work of the artist is both prophetic and time-less. It analyzes and confronts not only its own milieu but somehow manages to deal with issues that transcend the moment of creation. And, without question, God's work in the presence and teaching of Jesus in the world did not die on a Roman cross. In some mysterious, nearly indefinable way, he still lives on in our midst.

The Christian proclaimer also lifts up a timeless and prophetic message. The idea of an all-loving, all-forgiving God and all-loving, all-forgiving style of life for the Christian confronts our war-torn, materialistic age in the same way it confronted the era when B. C. became A. D. There is little doubt about the potential of mass media as a means of transmitting prophecy. However, the very nature of mass media is temporariness, the opposite of timelessness. Brevity, temporariness, and transience are common characteristics, shared by all mass media. They are gradually making easy and temporary change a way of life. Can the gospel message, that necessarily calls for ultimate and permanent change in both persons and society, be believed when it is transmitted via the transient mass media?

Finally, art requires a response. When art is art, it is impossible to avoid reacting to it. Before a painting, you can become speechless in the presence of its beauty, be repulsed by the ugliness of its message or shrug your shoulders in dismay and walk away. These, and many more, are all valid responses to art. The kind of response is not as important as the fact that the nature of the work is such that it cannot be ignored. God in the form of Jesus could not and cannot be ignored either. Some men call him Savior and Lord. Others execute him for criminal fraud.

And, if the Christian witness is presented with integrity and sincerity by a person whose life is a living demonstration of his faith, the message cannot be ignored. It can be rebutted, denied, or accepted but it demands a response of some kind. When witness takes place in a one-to-one confrontation, the opportunity for dialogical response between transmitter and receiver is possible. In most mass media situations, however, this kind of two-way communication is prohibitive.

Can the Christian embody something of himself in his message when transmitted via mass media? Can truth be conveyed and believed when transmitted over systems that are normally perceived as less than truthful? Is the highly transient nature of mass media conducive to prophecy and timelessness? Can response take place when proclamation of the gospel happens through mass media?

We must respond affirmatively to some of these questions and negatively to others. Still others are, in part and for the present moment, unanswerable. But, along with other similar questions they point to the fact that we cannot go about blindly assuming that mass media is the once and for all answer to mass evangelism.

On the other hand, mass media has become more than just a segment of our culture involved only in the transmission of information. To a large extent, mass media *is* our culture and therefore must be considered in any scheme of mass evangelism.

Consider, for instance, that 92 percent of the homes in the United States have one or more television sets viewed on the average of 6½ hours a day. More than a billion persons around the world participate in simultaneous live hook-ups of moon landings and funerals of world leaders.

In the United States, persons become absorbed in mass media culture at an early age. The average pre-schooler has watched 4,000 hours of television before he enters the first grade. Without question, he receives more input from mass media in this critical period than from any other single source. By the age of 18, the average transistorized teen-ager has watched a total of 16,000 television hours and listened to unmeasurable volume of radio hours. Upon graduation from high school, the average American child has spent twice as much time absorbing electronic images as he has spent in the classroom.

Print media is also filling up a growing share of our total culture. Twenty million magazines go into American homes every week and the paperback explosion has made books a two billion dollar a year mass medium. In addition, 110 million newspapers are read every day in this country alone and the median time spent by American adults reading newspapers is 52 minutes per day.

In an average day, we ingest between 20,000 and 50,000 words and thousands of highly symbolic visuals from magazines, books, radio, television, newspapers, signs, billboards, labels on cans, brochures, and other mass media. Nearly all of these words and images are prepared and presented by communications specialists backed up by high priced creativity and sophisticated research to help them impress messages on both our conscious and subconscious minds.

Mass media is rapidly becoming more than just an extension of man. It is quickly becoming a major force that is shaping our culture and influencing the formation of individual personality. Commercial and government interests are becoming highly sophisticated in the work of public temperature control via the manipulation of mass media images. Whether we like it or not and whether we do it well or not, we are compelled to investigate the potential for mass media witness. We must learn to use mass media before it uses us.

So, if proclamation via mass media is problematic and yet virtually a necessity, we must set out boldly to use the media in the best way we can. The problems must be overcome where they can and compensated for where they cannot be solved.

First, we must learn the subtleties of media dynamics and convert potential problems into assets. We have to isolate the problems and learn to understand them. In addition to the speculative problems isolated above, there are some basic problems connected with the very nature of mass media. For instance, how do you proclaim to the needs of a widely diversified audience? Manufacturers can isolate that segment of society that is their best market and focus their message on them. But the gospel is concerned for every human being and cannot be beamed at only one market.

Illiteracy is a significant roadblock to international proclamation because two thirds of the world's population cannot read, especially in those areas in which the only available mass media forms are newspapers and signs. In addition, there are 8⅓ million illiterates in the United States that must be considered in any mass media evangelism approach.

The individual tolerance to mass media exposure is also problematic. Radio network studies show a person's tolerance level for an uninterrupted radio message is less than 3½ minutes. Visual images increase the tolerance time for television viewing only slightly. Of an average of 560 advertising messages that assault an adult American every day, he notices only 70 to 80.

A fuller understanding of the peculiar nature of mass media communication will gradually help us to make an effective mass media witness.

Second, we must develop a new understanding of the nature of a modern pagan, the person who stands outside the faith. How does he think, talk, laugh and live? What are his needs, his anxieties, his fears? We cannot go into programs of mass media evangelism just assuming we fully understand the target audience.

Third, we must begin experimentation with mass media formats that attempt to solve some of the limitations such as one-way communication flow, diversified audience, built-in transience and low tolerance levels. For example, small mixed groups of Christians and pagans might be organized to meet at the time of a proclamation broadcast with the hope of providing vehicles for dialogue, response and experiential involvement on a person to person basis in direct correlation with the content of the transmitted message. Or, we might attempt broadcast "lobbying" to incorporate theological themes into ongoing dramas in which persons have already become experientially involved. Regular television programming frequently perpetuates the "folk religion" mentioned above. With some concrete effort at the sources of creativity and production, a call to national repentance could permeate many programs.

Fourth, we must become ecumenical. The overwhelming cost of mass media evangelism virtually demands a united effort. Furthermore, when the gospel is presented via mass media, there can be no brand names except Christian or the integrity of the message is in question.

Fifth, we must aim at experience as well as information. We have to develop methods of involving persons in experiencing God's love via mass media rather than trying to tell them about it. This is not an easy requirement but it may well be the most important one.

Sixth, we must develop a theology of anonymous proclamation and anonymous conversion. Too much of our witnessing is based on the ego needs of the proclaiming person or group. We have measured success not by qualitative changes in society but by counting noses at the altar. If mass media evangelism is to be successful at all, it will demand that we willingly allow credit to fall where it may, seeking only to convert persons and society to the will of God. The whole idea of membership in an institutional body may have to be moved down the line in importance to give mass media appeal integrity.

Finally we must consistently remember that the most powerful medium for transmitting the gospel is the warm-hearted Christian. Because the average American makes relatively intimate contact with more than 500 persons a month, the human animal is perhaps the most significant mass medium of all. And, without question, the loving action of God is best expressed through the loving actions and words of you and me, his disciples.

Questions for Reflection

1. What media are available for use by the church in my community?
2. What is my local church now doing to utilize media for proclamation in my community?
3. What might be accomplished through use of the mass media in my community?
4. How shall my local church respond to its media opportunities?

8

Key 73

By Ted Raedeke

Key 73 really resulted from a dream. In the Old Testament the prophet Joel predicted that in the latter day God's spirit would be poured out upon all men. That sons and daughters would prophesy. Young men would see visions and old men would dream dreams.

In 1967, Dr. Carl Henry, the editor of *Christianity Today*, had a dream. He projected this dream in an editorial in *Christianity Today* entitled, "Somehow Let's Get Together." Recognizing the urgency of the day and also knowing something about the need, Dr. Henry proposed that possibly Christians today could get together in order more forcefully and more fully to confront people with Jesus Christ. The editorial met with favorable response. And because of this, a meeting was held in Washington, or more specifically in Arlington at the Mariott Hotel located next to Francis Scott Key Bridge. Because of the location it was referred to as the Key Bridge Meeting. Forty-two churchmen were in attendance. They agreed that this had tremendous possibilities but they said this is not really our responsibility. This is the responsibility of the evangelism directors of the representative Protestant denominations. Future meetings were held for evangelism leaders until finally we came up with something on which we could agree. I'll share with you that some of the meetings were rather rough. There were times when I felt, "This is hopeless. It'll never happen!" But let's also remember that the spirit of God is still ruling in the church today and when we are led by his leadership, by his guidance and above all, when we ask for it, the Holy Spirit still has some surprises for us. Over a period

94

of several years the consultation grew. It was greatly enlarged and became pan-Christian—open for all who were interested to participate.

Key 73 was born and I am sure that under God it will be one of the greatest things that the church has experienced in our generation and possibly for several generations.

In order to avoid some pitfalls we immediately determined to keep the organizational structure, very, very simple. Too frequently we get bogged down in organization. I think we avoided this. There is a Central Committee consisting of one representative from each participating denomination or group. Presently we have over fifty denominations and groups representing approximately thirty million members committed to participate. At our last meeting in St. Louis seventy-three denominations and groups were represented. Hopefully we will exceed that number in commitment and participation when 1973 arrives. So, first of all there is a Central Committee. In addition to this there is an Executive Committee consisting of fifteen men elected by the Central Committee. In order to keep this entire movement on a sound financial basis there is a Finance Committee. Six resource committees have been established along with a Program Committee in order to formulate and to develop the thrust.

The objective of Key 73 is more forcefully and more fully to confront people with Jesus Christ by proclamation and demonstration, by witness and ministry. Both of these are necessary. Proclamation and demonstration should go hand in hand. It is a marriage not to be divorced. What God has joined together let not man put asunder! In evangelism we are concerned about relationships. First the vertical relationship with our God, then the horizontal relationship with our fellowman. Place these in proper perspective and you will shape them into the form of a cross. Where there is a cross there is Christ. Where there is Christ the mission of the church is being fulfilled.

Now when we speak of confronting people with Christ, I think of this post with which I am presently being confronted. And all I can say is that it stands in the way! There are forms of confrontation that do about the same thing. They get in the way.

There are some approaches that leave much to be desired. But generally speaking, in our confrontation of people with Jesus Christ, we must remember it is not only with lips, although this is the most common form of communication, but it must also be with life. Our lives must be a constant testimony of our faith in Christ. Paul says our lives are living epistles read by all men. Our lives must undergird our witness. Unless they undergird our witness, some may say, "What you are speaks so loudly I can't hear what you are saying."

Finally, our witness must be undergirded with our love. Among the early Christians the heathen, those outside their fellowship, could sneer at the story of the Resurrection, they could ridicule the story of the Crucifixion, but when they saw how these Christians loved one another they were drawn into their midst. The Lord predicted that in the latter day the love of many would wax cold. Possibly this is happening today, not only in the world but frequently also in the church. Let us love, not only in word, but also in deed. With this combination men will recognize the truth. This threefold confrontation with life, with lip, and with love might be compared to a three-legged stool. You remove any one of these and the witness is no longer complete. It falls! So also our witness fails. In all our evangelism activities we can do no better than to follow the example of our Lord who has commanded us to carry out our evangelism activities.

When we look at His evangelism ministry, we again find that it was threefold. First of all there was a direct evangelism approach. Person to person, eyeball to eyeball. We have many examples of this. Think, for example, of his confrontation with Nicodemus; the woman at the well of Samaria; Zacchaeus and others; even in the hour of death with the penitent malefactor. Today, if we wish to follow the Savior's example, we must be concerned about a personal confrontation. The Savior's personal confrontations produced much fruit.

Secondly, the Lord also practiced an indirect evangelism approach. And this, of course, was nothing more than his healing ministry, sometimes overlooked in our day by the church and by those who claim Christ. Never do we read that Christ was approached by anyone who was ever turned aside. Whenever he saw people in need he helped them. And today we cannot assume the stance as if to say, "I really don't care about your physical needs but if you are willing to hear about the gospel of Jesus Christ, I'll mouth that for you." It won't work!

Finally, there was a third evangelism approach and that was the Lord's directed evangelism approach. Namely sending the 12 and the 70. He chose men, trained men, and sent men. If a church is faithful to Christ and wishes to fulfill its evangelism responsibility, it must carry out a directed evangelism approach. So again, in order more forcefully and more fully to confront people with Jesus Christ, we today must follow the Lord's threefold evangelism approach—the direct, the indirect, and the directed confrontation.

Now what can we anticipate as far as Key 73 is concerned? There are three ways that you and I can anticipate being involved:

First of all, there are those things that *denominations will do separately*. Every denomination is charged with the responsibility of developing its own evangelism thrust for 1973. At no time will members of the Central Committee or Executive Committee dictate to participating denominations or groups precisely what shape or form their thrust should assume. This will not be done. This will be determined by the participating denominations. On the national level we plan to provide some resource material in order to share with participating denominations and groups what others are planning.

Secondly, there are those things that *denominations will do simultaneously*. We anticipate that there will be seasonal evangelism emphases during 1973 carried out by denominations and groups. And frankly, what happens in 1973 will depend largely on what happens in 1971 and 1972. Many denominations have declared 1971 as a year of *presentation*, 1972 as a year of *preparation*, and 1973 as the year of *penetration*. Not all denominations are using the same terminology for these years. We, for example in the Lutheran Church, Missouri Synod, this year are asking congregations to reevaluate what they are doing. Are they serving as an effective redemption center of God's Holy Spirit? Are the members of our church really mindful that they belong to this select fellowship of the redeemed, the concerned, and the sent ones? In our denomination, next year will be a year of mobilization. We will mobilize the laity, train them, and equip them for their ministry. I was happy to hear a previous speaker mention something about Luther. I like to think that Luther did away with laity, and made of every man a priest! Those who are God's priests must fulfill their ministry. Unfortunately, in many cases we have not equipped them for it.

Ultimately, 1973 will be a year of *confrontation* where members of our church, together with members of maybe one hundred other denominations and groups, will march forward, onward, and upward for Christ and for people. Our concern will be to bring Christ to men so that men might be brought to Christ.

Thirdly, there are those things that participating denominations and groups will do cooperatively, i.e. the use of the mass media and community confrontations.

Now, what do I envision in this regard? Let me share some of my personal thoughts. I don't know how many of these things will ultimately materialize, nor am I greatly concerned, because I am sure what emerges as we plan together will be best. This is the Lord's work, and the Lord is still ruling and guiding those who are concerned about Kingdom building.

I would like to believe that possibly on New Year's Eve, 1972, or New Year's Day, there could be a telethon involving well-known religious leaders. The purpose would be to project the message and the meaning of the gospel and to inform the world what Christians throughout the United States and Canada have planned for 1973. Basically, the purpose would be to inform, to witness, and to confront.

Then on the first Sunday in January, 1973 there might be a special order of worship used in all participating denominations. Think what it would mean to have all congregations throughout the United States and Canada using a common

order of worship. Impossible? Idealistic? Possibly I am an
eternal optimist, but I think it can happen.

We should encourage the artists, the hymn writers, the
sculptors, the painters to use their finest art and their best
skills for depicting the objectives of Key 73. And maybe some
of those prize hymns could be incorporated in that common
order of worship. Again, people will sing many things if they
know why they are singing them. Common melodies could be
found. Perhaps the front bulletin could depict the prize-
winning picture. Combined with this common order of worship there should be an opportunity for Christians to commit
themselves to the cause and specific tasks for 1973 might be
given. Whether this be in directed evangelism activity or
whether it be in some social ministry, there must be commitment if there is to be action.

Let me hasten to say that the entire effort must be undergirded with prayer. The Lord's condition still stands: "If my
people pray." Because, if God's people pray there will be
action! Prayer without action is hypocrisy. Action without
prayer is arrogance.

Then during the month of February there could be a personal confrontation of all members of the congregation to en-
list them for further activity. Perhaps a confrontation of the
people of the community could help build up a "responsibility"
list. How many people are there in the community who are in
need of the church's message and ministry? Maybe there
should be a Scripture distribution campaign. I hopefully anticipate group Bible studies where small groups would gather in
homes for a period of six weeks, possibly beginning the Thursday evening after Ash Wednesday and ending the Thursday
before Maundy Thursday. They might study the same lesson.
These are some of the things that might be incorporated in
Key 73.

Then Easter. Sometimes we have deplored some of the
activities of the young people during the Easter holidays. Why
not harness the energy of youth? Why not take advantage of
it? Why not have a rock festival during the Easter holiday
but make it a "rock of ages" festival? Thousands of young

people gathering for a specific purpose and that purpose is Christ.

On Easter Sunday, why not have a demonstration of Christians? Maybe in the village square, maybe in the city square, all singing, "I Know That My Redeemer Lives." Maybe encourage all Christians to use that original greeting, "He is risen," and the response, "He is risen indeed!"

During the period following Easter we might direct our concern toward the children. The holy writer said, "A little child shall lead them." Today, in "Christian" America 25 million children have no formal religious education. If America is to be more Christian tomorrow we had better begin today and begin with the children!

During the summer months we have an opportunity for ministry to the vacationers. From Thanksgiving until Christmas we might help people prepare for a more meaningful Christ-centered Christmas.

These are some of the things that I envision could, and maybe should happen during 1973. I am sure that when you start dreaming and others start dreaming there will be many more things to recommend. However, there is only one thing that can cause it to happen. The Apostle Paul refers to it in those six words which he addressed to the Christians at Corinth. "The love of Christ constraineth us." (2 Corinthians 5:14) Personally, I like the translation of the New English Bible where we read, "The love of Christ leaves us no choice." The activities of Key 73 planned, promoted, and prayed for leave us no choice because "the love of Christ constraineth us."

Questions for Reflection

1. In what examples of personal, indirect, and directed evangelism is my church engaged presently?
2. How can my local church expand its evangelism ministry to make it more responsive to the needs of all men?
3. How can my local church initiate responsible relationships with other churches of my denomination in my community for engaging in the task of evangelism? How can this be done with churches of other denominations?

81534

9

To Walk a New Road

By Joe Hale

I believe that fresh, daring, and presently undreamed of expressions of Christianity are about to burst forth. Through these we can experience—as never before in history—the impact of Jesus Christ and the force of the kingdom of God he announced. At least these are the signs I discern and I would agree with those who hopefully expect that just ahead of us lie the most opportune days of the church.

If we can discover the source of our life, if we can find unmistakable purpose given to us in Jesus, then we may begin to walk a new road—an exhilarating, rewarding, victorious road for us individually, but more importantly one that will blaze for all humanity a new future.

How different this road will be from the mundane, lackluster picture often conjured up by words like witness, cooperative evangelism, or mission.

These concerns are remote to many people. They are musty with past tradition and culture. They smack of *methods*—methods that were once mightily used—the census, an occasional evangelism meeting or ecumenical dialogue group, a joint Thanksgiving service—but which in recent years have either met with diminishing effectiveness or fallen into disuse as a waste of time.

We need to discover a far more exciting, and comprehensive concept of what it means to be an evangelist on a mission for God if we expect to make a serious bid for the commitment and loyalty of millions of Christians today who want to do the work of God, and to be sure that what they are doing really matters to the life of the world.

101

81534

Surely the new wine of the Evangel is not forever to be imprisoned in yesterday's wine skins! New avenues of witness are required if we arrest the attention of an increasing number of persons who do not attend churches or relate their lives to God in any way.

The mission of God in Christ is larger than one local church. It cannot even be accomplished by one denomination, no matter how large or strong, nor can it be directed by one cultural group or class of mankind. God's power does not reside in any single nation. Each of the six continents includes missioners to be sent and mission fields where persons wait to hear and heed the gospel. It is not geographical boundaries that ultimately separate us. We are divided by belief and unbelief; by commitment and indecision, by obedience and indifference.

And across these lines Christians proclaim the gospel—the good news that God offers every person a new creation, a second beginning. In both a shattering and a healing experience we may be claimed by God and begin to live through Christ. For God makes void our worship of the creature rather than the Creator, breaking the power of sin that grips us. He also heals our diseases. He desires to make us whole. This gospel has *evangelism* at its heart. Only as we cut a new way through our maze of confusion will we open a road men will take to find new life. The network of God's kingdom transcends every race, system of government, class, nation, or economic order. He calls all who will hear his voice to obey him.

I believe that Christians unitedly committed *can make a difference in life on this planet.* They can stand tall—looking over all separating fences to the far reaches of a global mission. All who trust by faith in Christ have a mandate to share this new life and to beachhead the purpose God has for men. This is an hour of destiny in which we live. We are moving in high gear toward decisions that will determine what our nation will be like—in its foreign policies, in its home crises, in its sensitivities to human need, and its response to human hurt. Christians have an unprecedented chance to make their faith explicit—compassionately, collectively, effectively—and thus shape the times through giving themselves for a cause—God's cause. The cost of involvement in our society is greater than ever before—far greater than in the era one hundred years ago when Christians often perceived their role in a passive sense. The great pulpiteers preached. The people listened.

We know today we must be the salt of the earth—not the salt of the church. And together, the whole Body of Christ can be the leavening influence in the world. Our very lives must cry out for the realization of Jesus' mission "to preach the gospel to the poor, to heal the broken hearted, and to preach deliverance to the captives, and recovering of sight to the blind, to set at liberty them that are bruised, to preach the acceptable year of the Lord."

The kingdom of God has to be realized in the streets, the factories, the homes—not in the institution of the church alone. Unless we are captured by this vision, God's mission revealed at Christmas, Good Friday, Easter, Pentecost will have failed—*with us!* If we are willing to separate cultural Christianity that dulls and often negates the gospel from the faith revealed in the New Testament *in our hearts and in our actions* we will then present with power the One who came as the Light of the nations and the Savior of the world.

We in the American Church stand at a point of crisis. When the Chinese write of "crisis," Alan Walker claims they use two characters: one for *peril* and the other for *opportunity*. We must make the barricade of peril, the threshold of opportunity! For when we are weak and afraid—or perhaps especially then —God makes his strength known through us! And at this crisis time we would not shrink from the conflict that rages within the world or within the church. We are torn between:

Folk religion and revealed Christianity,

Exclusiveness and inclusiveness,

Institutional encumbrance and freedom in the Spirit,

Unbelief and vital faith,

Secularism and belief in a living, active, Incarnate God,

Fragmentation of the Body of Christ and coordinated response to the purpose of God,

Religion as "getting" and religion as "giving."

When a local church spends as much annually to rent parking spaces for its staff as it gives for missions; when a women's society decides that the members should exchange gifts with each other at a Christmas party, but claims it must drop the support of a national pastor in India—then this attitude of "religion as getting" is amply illustrated.

Yet despite obstacles such as these, I have heightened hope for the tomorrows before us. As a river changes its course and cuts a new, more direct path toward the ocean, so in our time a new path is being formed for the mission of God to express itself. It is possible that we may fail God, letting his movement of redemption and reconciliation pass us by. But his kingdom, energized by that power which rolled the stone away from the tomb and raised Jesus from the dead, belongs to the future and it will not fail!

If a new course is being cut, how shall we recognize it? What are the marks that identify this new path of God's mission?

1. First of all, *it will center in the person of Jesus*. Jesus in his humanity made a perfect identification with us; in his love he showed the essential character of Love; in his compassion he demonstrated the one adequate "giving" life—a life of perfect obedience that led to death on the cross. After evil men did their worst—taking his life—God was faithful: He raised him from the dead to be alive for evermore! He pervades human history today. The distinctive event of his resurrected life makes Christianity a faith for today—an encounter with a living Person.

Those who move with God into the future will boldly confess that this man Jesus is the Christ of God, that since he has invaded our history, *potentially*, all things are new! He has already won the victory over principalities and powers. "He has made the forces of evil his prisoners of war, and publicly exposed them." He calls us to follow him and show in our lives, in our communities, and in our generation his coming kingdom. We own him as Lord *now* and look for the day when he will be acknowledged as the Lord of all history. But this conviction—Christus Victor—does not let us escape from involvement. On the contrary, we are thrust out to walk with Christ as co-laborers in building a new world.

2. Christians who take *the new path will relate the meaning of Jesus* to points of sensitive need in our world. If God created all men and equally loves each and every person, then no

TO WALK A NEW ROAD

condition of man, no unbridled nationalistic tendency, no conflict, war, or international misunderstanding is beyond his concern. The concern of this God who really deeply cares grips every follower of Jesus. The Christian, therefore, is motivated more basically and deeply than any other man. And, thus so motivated, he acts. He reaches out in flesh and blood compassion to all men. He embraces the total man. His physical need and spiritual health are inseparably intertwined.

When the indifferent and neglected, the wounded and the unbelieving see Christians sensitive to their hurts, understanding their bewilderments, caring for them, then and only then will they hear the gospel of Good News.

3. The new course for mission and evangelism *cannot be fenced in or restricted.* It is like the spirit of God that blows where it will. John Wesley said, "I look upon the whole world as my parish." And every Christian today sees "the world as his parish" in two senses. The "world" of ideas, movements, jobs, society, racial conflict, the world of the Spirit—all the "worlds" in which we move are related to the mission of God.

Then, the Christian is conscious of the total human scene —*the entire globe.* He sees the Body of Christ in its worldwide context. If the church is sick in America, he takes heart at its vibrant spirit in Latin America or parts of Indonesia. If the Gallup Poll continues to reveal that fewer and fewer people in our land are influenced by religion in general, or the church in particular, the Christian is encouraged that on the continent of Africa the most fantastic explosion of Christian faith in modern times is occurring. By the year 2000, one knowledgeable student of African culture predicts, 350,000,000 Christians will be living on that continent alone!

The plain fact is that those who walk the path of the future believe that Christianity has meaning for every person on the earth. If a new channel is cut in which missionary movement is reversed and begins to flow from the "non-Christian" East to the "Christian" West, those who see what is, with a world perspective, will not be disturbed. For *the* Mission is from God to *all* men—not *ever* from some men to other men! And for the Christian, loyalty to God who loved the world and gave his only begotten Son to redeem men and make of society a sign of his kingdom is greater than every other.

If the gospel is Good News it reaches out to hurricane victims in East Pakistan; it is a word for the Marxist in Russia; it speaks in judgment to the affluent materialist in America; and comforts the Asian mother who is crying because her baby is dead. It knows no lines of nation, color, education, or ideology. This gospel is the one universal. It has meaning for every single person.

4. The new path *will be marked by action, not theory*. This is already happening. Every time we move from the sanctuary of the church out into the street we find ourselves with other Christians—in the school, on the job, at the service club. Either we stand shoulder to shoulder in Christ's name bearing his cause, or we frustrate the will and purpose of God by erecting, or by default recognizing, man-made barriers. When our labels, denominational or otherwise, keep us from walking the road with others who name his Name, they are demonic and cause us to fail Christ at what may possibly be the most crucial time in our generation.

When God came in Jesus, there was an *Incarnation*. The Word became flesh.

God's divine mission is "incarnational" in style today. It is done in a specific place. It happens through a flesh and blood person. There is a moment in history and no ideal occasion or time exists for God to send another. The time is now! Now, he commissions us to live out the plan he instigated when he "broke down the middle wall of partition between us" on the hill of Golgotha.

The call to evangelism, specifically cooperative evangelism, may have extensions of meaning on levels other than local towns, communities, and specific cities—but one thing is sure —without persons in given places determining to bear witness unitedly for the sake of Christ, cooperative *action* will never happen.

This is why the concept of *Key 73* has so much potential. *Key 73* is not primarily concerned with the church talking to the church, but is an expression of God's mission to the world. It is the church offering the Good News to secular man caught in the throes of success and prosperity, uncertainty, doubt, and failure.

As Christians individually and collectively bring resources of faith and courage and plunge forward, there may be born through *Key 73* a new era of Christian witness and a new penetration of God's rule in the lives of men in North America.

I am convinced that God is offering to us in the United States and Canada an unprecedented hour for evangelistic witness. Faithfulness demands our intense prayer, our serious thought, and our careful planning. What happens on this continent in 1971, 1972, and 1973 may trigger a movement of Christian advance that will extend like a tidal wave around the entire globe.

But this word of caution: *Key 73* will never happen in a national office, although a national office is in existence in St. Louis. It *may* happen if someone person, or group of people—laymen, pastors, or youth take the initiative to open the door for a united witness. But someone has to take the first step. This is not only a challenging opportunity for us to break through with new forms of evangelism, but more basically, it is a test of our faith—our faith in God, our faith in ourselves, and our faith in others. It will test our confession that we are a fellowship of believers.

At this time when the nerve of mission seems to have been cut by a lack of confidence within the church, is it possible we may be used of God to help rekindle faith within our nation? We can if pointedly, specifically, and openly we invite other Christians to walk with us, or *perhaps more importantly*, we walk with them the road of witness beginning with 1973.

I keep asking the question: Will we as individuals and as a denomination initiate new action in evangelism where we live? What will we do? We will be less than faithful if we merely look back to other eras, to other historical epochs for tried and true models of evangelism, left-overs in the arsenal of the past.

God calls us to mount a new offensive today. Where it will eventually end, none of us know. But take the new path, we must! In our most hopeful vision we see a new birth of vital Christianity on this continent in our lifetime. Our minimal impulses whisper, at least, that we can be catalytic influences used by God to stir new passion and compassion in the church, that her alabaster box may be broken afresh in the market place of the world.

The possibility of our uniting with other Christians in *Key 73* affords us a new opportunity for a cooperative response. It can take two shapes: One, for the sake of survival throws up the sandbags to save the town from the flood. It is preventive and geared to avert the threat. But there is another kind of co-operation—the kind that put men on the moon. It is adventurous and aims for the future.

If survival evangelism is all we see in our vision, let's forget it and do something more exciting. Survival evangelism will neither evangelize nor will it save the institution of the church. Only as we lose ourselves in some undreamed of pioneering venture will we find the new road. For only in costly commitment will we stand near the spirit of Jesus who dared to give his life for us that we should no longer live for ourselves.

Questions for Reflection

1. What is an evangelist?
2. How can I expand my own role as an evangelist?
3. How can my local church become more effective in its evangelism ministry?
4. What does "Kingdom of God" mean in my life and my community in the here and now?

10

PRAYER

By Albert C. Outler

Almighty God, our heavenly Father, who in thy great mercy hast promised comfort and guidance and insight and strength to all who grope and seek, give us now a new sense of the time of our lives in which thou hast called us to thy service; a new awareness both of the dangers and of opportunities that crowd in upon us; a new sense of our own desperate need of thy grace and illumination; a new sense of thy Holy Spirit's regnant presence in our lives; a new sense of Christ's love and mercy.

For all the things we strive to do that are consonant with thy will, multiply and fructify our best intentions. For all those good intentions which are still corrupted with our self-interest and our blindness, which blockade and thwart even our best ambitions, give us a new sense of our dependence on thy correcting wisdom; a new sense of reliance; a new sense of trust—that in all of our deliberations begun, continued, and ended in thee, we may always be assured of thy guidance and of thy grace.

Our hope is that in our time, in ways that are beyond our own abilities, we may be enabled to serve thee in thy kingdom. In these tremendous efforts of imagination represented here and in these projects under discussion in this group, make each one of us a prophet, each one of us a priest, each one of us a witness to thy love: so that without either timidity or brazen pride we may open ourselves to thy guidance and to the leadership of thy Spirit. All in the name of Jesus Christ our Lord. AMEN.

NOTES

LINCOLN CHRISTIAN COLLEGE AND SEMINARY

NOTES